Little Molly

by

Rosemarie Smith

**Grosvenor House
Publishing Limited**

This book is published by
Grosvenor House Publishing Ltd
28-30 High Street, Guildford, Surrey, GU1 3HY.
www.grosvenorhousepublishing.co.uk

A CIP record for this book
is available from the British Library

ISBN 978-1-907211-58-4

This is the true story of a little girl who battles to keep her younger brothers and sister alive.

Rosemarie Smith

Acknowledgement

Had it not been for the following people my story would never have been told._

My Counsellor Clive Powell: thank you for your patience, optimism and insight.

Elaine Palmer and Wendy Kopetzki who spent countless hours typing and correcting my errors: many thanks to you both.

To John Edwards, Julie, Steve, Danny and Kirsten for showing me that some of life's precious moments are shared with friends closest to us.

To Ruth Pulis, Maggi Taylor and all the staff at Grosvenor House Publishing for their speed when replying to my emails, for their patience when answering my questions and for their professionalism when piecing my book together: many thanks to you all.

And finally, a kind and loving thought for my children Ian, Cheniel, Kyle, and Allishia who have shown me that despite my abusive childhood life can still be beautiful.

Foreword

I would like to say I enjoyed writing this book, but it wouldn't be fair to say I did it without a struggle. When I accepted this challenge I must admit I didn't think I would find my story so hard to tell and there was no one more surprised than I, when I finally wrote the last page. It was only when I wrote Molly that I could faithfully acknowledge to myself the true devastation of child abuse. When you feel a victim of child abuse it is extremely difficult to look upon the past with compassion or understanding, as guilt totally devours our minds. So until I wrote my story down and read it like an outsider looking in, it was impossible to understand how destructive the abuse had been.

Having re-read the whole story of Molly from beginning to end, I can now see the saddest part of my life was accepting abuse as normal. Although I still haven't been able to understand why this happened to me, the writing of Molly has helped me to move on with my life, accepting that it did happen but will never stand in **my way again. The story of Molly will always stir the saddest of memories that I have of my childhood – even so I will look back at** it completely satisfied that writing it was the best step forward. With a tremendous amount of help and support from my counsellor Clive Powell, I have completed the most difficult journey of my life and I thank him for accompanying me.

When I look back at my childhood I remember all the years I suffered in silence, thinking about all the people I could have told, but didn't. Then I wonder how many thousands are still waiting, desperate to tell their story - my heart goes out to them. It's difficult to face up to an abuser and the truth is it doesn't get any easier with age. But, luckily, we have people like Clive and it is people like him that make a difference. I would like to take time to pay tribute to my children Ian, Cheniel, Kyle, and Allishia who at times have suffered from the result of my upbringing. I thank them from the bottom of my heart for having patience and understanding and for allowing me to experience true love and happiness. Thanks, kids I love you and I have always loved you.

Molly's Prayer

Where do you come from? I am so unsure
My eyes do not see you, but do you see me, Lord?
I do not understand, my mind will not accept
My family has forsaken me, and they have no regrets.
I have no friends, yet I yearn for many.
Pray Lord who will love one so melancholy,
Whose heart breaks, whose tears flow
I know not real love, how can that be so?
I am here Lord, all alone, can you not see?
There is nothing left on this earth, for a little girl like me.
How will I know you when you come to take my hand?
Will you ease away my pain, hold me close and comfort me?
In this cruel world I see little hope for me;
An innocent child; Suffering miserably!

Author's Notes

I have written this book to the best of my ability, upon memory only. Although I have written a reasonable amount I have decided to omit certain things for the sake of my family. If however, I have offended anyone I apologise most sincerely.

The story of a little girl called Molly

This is the true story of Molly, a seven-year-old girl who battles to keep herself, her younger brothers and her sister alive following abandonment by both her parents. Molly teaches her younger siblings to forage, scrounge and steal in an attempt to survive, while she suffers both physical and severe sexual abuse from her older siblings. Just as things begin to go wrong for Molly and her young family, her prayers are answered.

CHAPTER 1

The Beginning

I lived with my parents and nine other siblings in a three bedroom council house at Beech Crescent, Eckington, a small mining village situated on the Yorkshire and Derbyshire border line. Our family home was both desolate and unmanaged, yet we had a huge flowerbed and vegetable garden, lovingly tended by my father, whose pride and joy were his dahlias. The garden was more orderly than our home ever was. The strongest memories of childhood with my parents are of a cold, dismal house, cluttered with items of no use; ashes from an unlit fire scattered over a large area of our kitchen; grease and dirt smeared across the white, enamel - topped table that stood beside the old gas cooker that was much the worse for wear; piles of unwashed crockery lay on a slimy, wooden draining board, while heaps of potato peelings stood in un - drained, stagnant water blocking the sink. Large piles of urinated blankets and sheets were thrown in an area beside the sink giving out a strong foul smell of ammonia that stuck in the back of my throat. Clothing we once wore was now laying around covered in mould and mildew, no longer fit for us to wear. Our kitchen was a horrific sight for anyone. However, little did we know, there was much worse to come.

My day usually began each morning when I was left alone to look after my younger brothers Andrew and Simon and my younger sister Lorraine, all who were under the age of six. Our bedclothes consisted of a couple of urinated, shabby blankets that I'd retrieved from beneath the kitchen sink along with a few of Father's old overcoats. The mattress we slept on was heavily stained with large patches of wet and dried urine that had been previously caused by our older siblings as well as ourselves and absolutely reeked ammonia. The bed was large enough to sleep the four of us, it had belonged to Mother and Father when our family lived together – the sleeping arrangements had been different then, as we each had our own places. But for now I slept in my heavily stained dress in the bed that everyone else had once slept in. All our clothes carried a strong smell of urine from previous night's bed wetting as we no longer had a change of clothing and never bathed. Our circumstances had become so desperate, clean laundry was no longer an option.

—◦◦◦—

My name was Molly. I was around seven years old, small and thin with dark bobbed hair. I was pretty, but I had become a foul – mouthed tomboy and spent all of my time fighting and hanging around the streets with my brothers.

I was one of ten children and certainly the oddest amongst them. Apart from my desire to roam with them from one end of the town to the other, I had absolutely nothing in common with any of them. I had three older sisters, the youngest being eight years my senior, and five brothers whose ages ranged from six months to nineteen years. Anne was the eldest and Simon was our baby, although, my youngest sister Lorraine fitted that role too.

I was the seventh child to be born after my brothers John, David, and Trevor and sisters Anne, Julie and Carol. Somehow I'd been caught up in the middle with groups of three all around me. Anne, Julie and Carol rarely tolerated my presence and for reasons unknown to me I wasn't accepted as readily as they accepted each other. I didn't fit in as well as I should have and always knew that somehow I was different. Julie spent a lot of her time in a convalescent home. It was suggested by the local authorities that she might benefit from different surroundings as they were convinced the rash she was totally covered in was the effect of a nervous disorder. I didn't see her that much. I remember crying when they took her away, but it seemed that, after a while, time naturally healed and I began to forget her. Anne lived and worked in Hathersage so only came home at weekends. She had spoken so often about leaving home and was delighted when she finally heard that the Slatteries family had accepted her as their nanny.

John however remained a home bird and worked on Wards farm. He was courting June, their daughter. Since his release from the institution for young offenders he found it difficult to get work anywhere else so found working on the farm convenient. He more or less worked when he felt like it just to prove he was his own boss. He hated authority and rebelled against everything that represented it. The rest of us were too young to leave home and had never, up to this point, experienced being away from it.

My mother spent most of her time away from our house working long hours in factories or enjoying a social life in the public houses. We rarely saw her. My father had recently fled our home after a desperate argument that became violent. It had been the only time I had seen him lose his temper. Prior to that, I had always known him to be a lovely man. I knew how much he cared for us so I hadn't expected him to leave. I was devastated when he did. Losing the security of our parents left me feeling responsible for my younger siblings. My father still occasionally visited our home, but I found his visits short and upsetting. He and Mother no longer enjoyed being in each other's company so violent arguments broke out each time he came. Every one of us cried when he left the house but it made so little difference to Mother. She carried on living her life without him, regardless of our feelings. She spent most of her time with her friends, away from the house and away from us. At first she was gone for days, then the days became weeks, and the weeks became months, making me feel so unhappy I sometimes wished I hadn't been born.

John took charge of the home, what was left of it. He had always been the strong figurehead of the family, even when Father had been at home. Yet, Father was a much gentler character and was never accepted by John as his peer. This caused arguments between them. Father was so afraid of John. He would cower when he came near him and tended to give in to him easily. For some reason John was much more violent than any of us and didn't mind taking his anger out on Father, or anyone else for that matter. He had a strange personality that frightened everyone, family and outsiders alike, he was always losing his friends because of it and even the friends he managed to keep showed their fear of him.

Carol was the closest person to John. She knew him better than any of us and spent a lot of her time socializing, going to pubs and clubs and getting drunk with him. They both shared the same friends and had much in common - they were inseparable. Even so, she was insistent that she feared him just as we all did.

As each member of our family left the house, circumstances for me and my younger siblings became desperate. John found David and Trevor part time work on Wards farm just a few miles away from our home. Carol slowly drifted away from us and went to lodge with her boyfriend and his relatives. This resulted in me being left alone to fend for three younger siblings. My mother's visits to the house had now become so infrequent I never expected to see her again. I had totally given up on my father as no one mentioned him anymore. My parents had been separated for some time and showed they were unwilling to be reconciled, leaving the whole family heartbroken.

After spending weeks in our house alone, it began to look like a dumping site. We had no gas, electricity, or fire for warmth and I couldn't remember the last time we ate. Time slowed and I began to worry. The pain of hunger got the better of me. I became so frightened I wondered what was going to happen to me. I knew we had to eat and as time passed I felt so desperate that my survival instincts kicked in and I began to rummage through neighbours' dustbins searching for food. Occasionally I found pieces of uncut bread and over-ripe fruit covered in grime and wet ash. There were times when I found food I couldn't identify but still, I felt so hungry

I carelessly filled my gut with it. I hadn't eaten for so long that the thought of my younger siblings joining me threatened my very existence. Selfishly I left them to their own devices, only realising after a few days that if I didn't allow them to eat alongside me, they might die. Our local Co-op store became the family's main target and at times I rummaged their bins and stole food and sweets from the shop. Their bins were large and held more food, but there was a knack to getting it out. I demonstrated to my younger siblings, the precise technique of using the adjacent wall to aid the ascent up and onto the rim of the metal bins. There was a delicate art of balancing, ensuring that we didn't fall either into the rotting, festering mounds of food or back onto the concrete slabs below. I showed them how to steal sweets without getting caught. I knew it was wrong but it was the only way I knew how to keep them alive.

My brothers returned from the farm late at night bringing potatoes and duck eggs that the farmer had given them. When he wasn't so generous, they stole them. They came home around midnight tired and hungry occasionally bringing two shillings; one for the gas and one for the electricity meter which enabled me to cook their suppers. If I didn't make too much of a fuss at being woken up in the early hours, I was rewarded with a fried duck egg. It was something I looked forward to despite being woken from my sleep. The eggs were huge, almost as big as the pan. They filled the kitchen with the tastiest aroma I knew; I couldn't wait to tuck in.

Each day became more difficult, the days were long and it became harder to find enough food for the four of us. My younger siblings spent time crying and constantly complained of hunger. Simon cried most of the time and

I would spend my day carrying him around, rocking him in my arms trying to induce sleep. But when the going got tough and I got scared, I cried too.

I couldn't bear being in the house on my own, I was frightened and the fear of being forgotten seemed to overpower everything so I took my siblings on long walks looking for food. We scrumped apples from local orchards and stole rhubarb from neighbours' gardens as we had exhausted our own long ago. We picked succulent berries from the brambles hoping they weren't the poisonous kind that Mother had warned us about and chewed on the stalks of a fennel plant that Father had once shown us, it didn't fill our stomachs but the taste of aniseed was delicious. Some days I'd drag my siblings all the way to town looking for lost coins or scraps of food we could scrape up off the floor and any that had been thrown into the gutter. The chip shop was our favourite haunt where we begged scraps of food and picked up yesterday's newspapers that had the remainder of fish and chips still stuck to them. We pulled out sweet papers and ice cream cartons from bins outside the shop, licking and eating anything that was stuck to them. It was usually late and very dark when we made our way home. Even the shortest way back seemed too long and we cried and sniffled as we struggled to get home. I carried Simon in my arms passing folks along the way; too drunk to be concerned, they never raised an eyebrow. I prayed for Mother's return while we'd been gone, but my prayers were never answered.

Wherever we wandered, no matter how far we walked, we always made it home before our brothers returned from the farm. I realised the shilling they had put in the electric meter the night before had run out, leaving our house in total darkness. This was a time I felt most vulnerable, so I cried as I clung to my siblings whilst climbing the stairs to our bedroom. We snuggled into bed and covered our faces with enough coats to weigh down our fears and hid ourselves from the dark, hoping the imaginary beasts that invaded our minds would eventually allow us to sleep.

I remember there were many days when we had walked all day long but still didn't find anything to eat, so I began to steal from neighbours. I found that if one of my siblings helped me, I was able to climb through pantry windows into larders to steal food. I passed lots of food through the windows to my siblings trying hard not to get caught, but often peeling the skin from my thighs as I tried hurrying out of the windows. I never cried until I was clear of getting caught as my fear numbed the pain until I knew I was safe. The large selection of preserves and warm pies that had been stored to cool looked so good I couldn't resist the temptation of stuffing my mouth full before I left, then through sheer excitement I told my siblings, what it was that I saw and everything I ate. Although I was terrified of getting into trouble the smell of food drifting through the air encouraged my frequent return to their homes. Sometimes the food smelt so good I wallowed in self pity. I could never remember food smelling as good as that.

Andrew and Lorraine soon learned how to steal without getting caught and stole packs of dried dates from the Co-op. They were a firm favourite of ours and once we found where they were stored we all stole as many as we could. Frank was the manager of the Co-op and knew our family well; he occasionally showed pity and gave Andrew large bags of over-ripe fruit for us to share.

Andrew chuckled with excitement when he brought food home, it seemed to give him a sense of importance. He understood the need to spread our food out so only allowed us a single piece of fruit, when he felt the need to eat. There had been so many times when we gave no thought to tomorrow and as a result we had often been without for days. So, when Andrew took charge, he took his role seriously and did it quite well. Frank had often filled bags with over-ripe bananas, apples and oranges that he'd carefully selected from the fresh fruit boxes on the shelves then gave them to us. He had done this even when Mother had been at home, knowing we were the largest and poorest family on the estate. We learned from an early age to eat what we could when we could. Even when our family were together, there were many days when we went without.

Frank knew we stole from the shop but often turned a blind eye. Other staff chased us away as it had become so regular it interfered with their work and often offended their customers, but that didn't deter me. I had lived on stolen sweets and food from the Co-op from as far back as I could remember, the only difference being that I came to depend on it.

—⁓—

CHAPTER 2

A Cruel Streak

On occasions, Carol came home to check on us and to see if Mother had been back. We went wild with excitement the minute we saw her as it was usually so long since we'd had any family contact, our emotions just poured out. She came with her boyfriend Barry, carrying a modest bag of groceries that consisted of potatoes and tomato soup. It was a very special time for us as she cooked mashed potato and soup for our dinner. It was the first meal we'd had cooked for us for months but as we tucked into it, no questions were raised on how we had managed to live or eat while she had been gone and none on how we were going to survive once she had left. It seemed once we were out of sight we were out of mind.

Carol wasn't always the best person to have around but it felt better than being alone. She was violent and quick-tempered, generally ordering me to clean up the house, often thumping me on the head and swiping me across my face. She threw pans, knives and forks out of anger, shouting and swearing but somehow the joy of having someone about the house over-rode my fear of her and encouraged a little happiness. Sometimes she kicked me in my stomach so hard I was knocked to the floor yet my instincts were always to forgive her. I tried to protect myself by holding my head tight with both hands but she found great pleasure in forcing me to remove them while she hurled abuse and threw more punches in my face. I reluctantly obeyed every command she made only to receive more punches that did more damage than the first.

She rubbed her hands afterwards, accusing me of injuring herself through beating me; failing to understand her injuries were self inflicted. I cried out but she forced me to stop, threatening me with more beatings if I didn't. My lips were cut and swollen and my nose was bleeding profusely, but the sight of blood made no difference to her and a few hours later she behaved like she'd done nothing at all. I couldn't think what it was that Carol didn't like about me as there had been many times when she had been so nice to me. Thinking back, I could remember Mother punching Carol as hard as she punched me but, I couldn't understand the reason for that either. Despite her faults, Carol, at that time was the only security we had; she was the only one that remained close to home so we looked forward to seeing her. There had been many times I had hoped she would stay and look after us but come nightfall she left the house alongside Barry, leaving us all on our own, while we were in bed asleep.

During their short visits, Barry pulled handfuls of loose change from his pockets and threw it onto the floor, knowing my siblings and I would fight over it. It became a standard joke between them so, for a while they rolled around with laughter, amusing themselves at our desperation but they failed to realise the money they frequently cast aside helped keep us alive. Once they had left, we pooled the money together to buy food for when we felt hungry. Barry carried a strong smell of beer on his breath and spoke with a slur but he was so much kinder than Carol, and we loved him anyway. He often tried to stop Carol from beating me, but she carried on regardless. Although I think his ingratiating pleading lessened the power she enforced behind the beatings, he still wasn't strong enough to override her.

Barry had always shown kindness to my younger siblings and occasionally took them out for a treat while I was forced to stay and clean up our house. As they left I followed, hoping Carol would allow me to go with them but this just gave her more excuses to beat me. I reluctantly turned back crying, feeling hurt and alone knowing they would be gone all day. I was so afraid of being in the house on my own I lost all confidence to care for myself. When our house was empty, I felt vulnerable and spent the whole day crying, wishing for Mother, wondering, if she would ever come home. I cried all evening as I cleaned the house and again when I went to bed. I was nothing without my siblings; when they were here they gave me the will to take care of myself and all the strength I needed to take care of them, but without them I was lost. I spent the whole night crying until I fell to sleep, but when I woke the following morning, I found my siblings sleeping at the side of me as if the previous night had never happened. The early morning sun was shining through the window and silence ruled our house, no sign of Carol and Barry, and our dogs still sleeping at the bottom of our beds.

Every morning was the same; I wandered downstairs, hoping to find Mother and Father sat in our kitchen, just like they used to be, but each morning my hopes were shattered. I was greeted with the same old mess that covered our sink and kitchen table, giving out that strong foul smell that lingered on my hair and in my clothes. I looked around, paying particular attention to the large pile of black wellington boots and old shoes that belonged to my family, clumsily hung from the wall cupboard beside the sink and pairs of Mother's old shoes that had been chewed by our dogs and abandoned in the middle of the kitchen floor. I noticed empty food cans with sharp, ragged edges thrown on the draining board and discoloured potato peelings left in the sink to rot. It was Carol's, way of taking care of herself. She was almost sixteen years old and clearly took a leaf from my mother's book – visiting our house occasionally. She cooked herself something to eat before she fed us with any food that remained, and then ordered me to clean any mess that she made before I went to bed. Then she walked away from our house just as Mother did without any feelings of guilt or remorse.

Carol was cunning, she never forgot to ask if Mother had been home since her last visit, but I knew her well and understood the meaning to her question. She wanted to know if Mother had left any money since she had seen me last. Carol called at our house intermittently to collect every penny which was left by Mother and to spend the shillings my brothers left for the gas and electric meters. I was usually very careful and hid what I didn't want her to have but she knew when I lied and beat the hell out of me until I gave in to her. My older brothers, spent most of their time at the farm and knew I was terrified of the dark so entrusted me with the two shillings they'd put aside for the meters, confident they'd have cooking facilities and light when they came home but, when Carol called, she didn't think twice about taking them. She had left us in the dark so many times my brothers eventually decided to hide the shillings before they went to work knowing I couldn't hand them over to her.

She had already exhausted our little green Co-op book that gave us instant credit, so we couldn't use it again until the debt had been cleared. She had purchased very little food for us on her visits back home but bought much more for Barry's relatives to help pay for her own keep whilst living with them. I often saw her purchase carrier bags full of food and cigarettes with our green book, then, walk away from us paying no attention to our desperately sad faces or hungry cries. I watched her many times catching a bus to Stavely where she lived with Barry, taking all the food with her.

Most Fridays, Mother called at our house to leave a little money for Carol so she could purchase groceries and put a shilling in our gas and electric meters. But being who she was Carol bought a small amount of groceries then socialised with the rest, leaving us without food for the rest of the week. I remember she never forgot to buy herself a new supply of cigarettes and the occasional bottle of hair spray to do up her hair, but never gave us anything more than she had to.

My eldest sister, Anne, was a little more thoughtful and came home some Friday nights with a box of fancy buns that she had purchased on her way home. She always asked if Mother had been back, then contacted her via the telephone that stood at the corner of our street. Although she never allowed us to speak to her, she made it clear to me it was Mother. They made arrangements to speak at specific times each Friday evening but it seemed the call never lasted long and we never had the chance to speak to her.

Afterwards, Anne dressed to go socializing with her boyfriend as if nothing had happened. Ron picked her up outside our house at the usual time of 8:00p.m, taking Simon with them. She brought new baby clothes and socks for Simon, knowing the clothing she brought the week before wouldn't be fit for him to wear. She wore large flouncy dresses that were fit for a queen. Everything she did was routine, although she spent a lot of time dressing and doing her hair,she still spared a little time for us before going out.

Anne was beautiful; she had lots of patience and spent time playing the piano for us, until she left the house. We had a beautiful piano in our front room that only Anne could play. When Mother and Father where still together and we lived as a proper family she taught me to sing my first song; The B.I.B.L.E; then she taught Andrew and Lorraine and when we went to Sunday school we all sang it together. Anne liked to play the piano; she was fluent and loved to hear me sing, it was always a happy time when we were together. But when Ron called to take them out, Andrew, Lorraine and I returned to the streets in search of food, never giving up our fight for survival, looking for new haunts in the hopes of staying alive. I knew Anne would spend the whole weekend with Ron and his family not far from our house so I didn't feel entirely alone.

My older siblings had lots of people they could approach for help but we had no one and nowhere to go and although I knew they were still close by; they might well have been a million miles away. Sunday afternoon, Anne left for work around 4:30p.m. Being a nanny, she didn't always get home at weekends so we never knew when we'd be seeing her again. There had been so many times when she took the weekends off and hadn't even called to see us, knowing we were still on our own. Some weeks we didn't see anyone. There were days when I felt so desperately hungry I thought I would die before I saw anyone again. My siblings cried out with stomach cramps and I begged food from people in the streets, but following hours of humiliation I gave up and cried too. I don't know if I cried for myself or my siblings but my tears ran down my cheeks as freely as I breathed in air. I was a child yet I felt responsible for their hunger, their pain and their worst fears. For every day that went by, our circumstances became more desperate and I wasn't sure we were going to make it.

I wasn't able to read or write but I was willing to try anything to keep us alive. I remembered the little green Co-op book that Carol used to purchase cigarettes and food when she had no money, so I scribbled onto the pages like Carol had done in the past; ordering food on credit. I hadn't the nerve to take it to Frank myself just in case my scribble was rejected with a stern telling-off, so I sent Andrew and Lorraine who didn't know any better. They had no idea my scribble wasn't for real and called out for me to order sweets like Mother had, in the past. I said I would, then, prayed for it to work just for them. But I wasn't confident. I handed them the book with several lines of scribble on one page and allowed them to walk across to the Co-op happy and full of excitement, but when they handed the book to Frank he laughed and sent them home. They were in floods of tears when it didn't work so, I tried a second time amending the scribble a little. It had been the only time in my life that I'd wished that I could write. On my final attempt, Frank showed concern and walked back to our house alongside Andrew and Lorraine. He knew something was wrong!

When he reached our house, he handed me the book and asked where Mother was. We stood huddled together and shrugged our shoulders. For some reason I felt a need to protect her and fell silent, terrified of people finding out we had been left on our own; I glared at my siblings hoping they wouldn't say a word but, I think he knew. A while later when he had closed the shop, he returned to our house with a large bag of overripe fruit suggesting it might tide us over until Mother came home; then winked at me as he walked out the door.

Some mornings when I woke it seemed I would cry for hours. I found it hard to entertain my younger siblings, being left alone in the house made them cry most of the day so I sang songs and played games to try and take their minds off Mother, but it didn't always work. We had no clean clothes to change into and I dressed Simon in dirty towels in place of nappies, but his excrement still dropped to the floor as I carried him. I didn't know how to toilet train so I found it difficult to care for him. I wrapped soiled blankets around him enabling me to take him to the park but the park was a good, long walk through our estate and down long water-pitted lanes, and past rows of slag heaps, but it took our minds off being alone. On the way down we picked up food that had been dropped and took advantage of Nightingale's sweet shop, from which we stole regularly. We stole bottles of milk and orange juice that had been left on neighbours' doorsteps by the milkman and drank it on the way. This way we didn't feel hungry during the day.

We spent time playing with the piglets that were penned opposite Nightingale's shop, fed a horse with the grass that we picked from the verges along the wayside and typically spent hours throwing stones at derelict buildings. I knew we shouldn't have but it seemed such good fun. Our visits to the park were a daily routine and although we chose to vary the route, we caused dreadful havoc whichever way we went.Unlike my older siblings, we little ones had lived in this area all our lives, but still knew it wasn't free from danger for children like us. I recall a particular day when we made the same journey at approximately the same time as we always had, but this time we saw a rather ugly looking fellow riding up and down the lane on his moped. Crowds of children were begging him for a ride. But then he paused at the top of the lane, a little way from where I stood. I got excited when he offered a ride to me. I stood mesmerized for a while, until eventually he asked me again. Thinking how exciting it would be, I accepted without giving it a moment's thought. I didn't know him, although I could remember seeing him on our estate, but the other children seemed relaxed with him, so I went ahead climbing up onto the bike and sat on the seat behind him, wondering where to put my feet. Suddenly he pulled my arms around his middle and told me to hang on tight. As the bike's engine started to roar the other children laughed and I began to scream wholeheartedly. The bike built up speed as we sped down the lane, avoiding the water-pitted holes and he raced to the bottom where I expected him to turn and ride back again, like he'd done with so many others but he turned to the left and rode down lanes I wasn't familiar with, until we approached a small thicket. He rode the bike as far as he could into the dense thicket and then told me to get off. I was scared and did as he said. He took off his helmet, climbed off the bike and pulled it back onto its stand. I remember I wanted to cry as I focused on his unusual maroon tainted face but I couldn't. I knew what he was going to do even before he ordered me to lay on the floor but I was so frightened I couldn't speak. I had experienced this sort of thing with my brother John, so I associated it all with hate and violence. I had learned that time passed much more quickly if I didn't struggle, so I laid down on the floor and turned my head away so I didn't have to look at him, feeling nothing but the pain he was causing me. I trembled as he rubbed furiously at my vagina. Wasting no time,he climbed on top of me with the whole weight of his body against mine, forced his penis inside me and ejaculated. I lay quite still wondering what he was going to do with me. His aggressive breathing had stopped and he was silent, but as he removed his short, overweight body from mine, he looked down at me in disgust as he rearranged my clothes. Then allowing me to my feet, he looked at me as if I was nothing.

Although it was a bright summer's day, I felt cold and trembled with fear. My legs where paralysed and I could barely move but in time I struggled to make my way out of the thicket. I wanted to run and get away from him but as I tried to move forward the whole of my body froze, holding me back. I tried to scream but I had no voice and the only thought I had was, 'Why me?'

There were lanes upon lanes all around the thicket with slag heaps as high as mountains. As I stood and looked around tears streamed down my face, as suddenly my thoughts turned to Mother and just for a second I hated her. He pulled his bike to the side of me and ordered me to climb back on. Too frightened not to I did as he said. Kicking up the mud with his wheel, he drove me back up to the top of the lane where he had first seen me. With every muscle in my body shaking, I climbed from his bike wondering why I was still alive.

I had been gone for so long there were no children waiting at the top of the lane and my siblings had gone on without me. I felt I was to blame and hated myself for it. I was unhappy and all I wanted to do was rid myself of the pain. I cried at the thought of my mother not being there when I needed her most and convinced myself it wouldn't have happened if she had been there. For the first time ever I hated the place, I was sad and lonely and full of pain - I could think of nothing but her. As he rode away I felt my breath release and I began to cry as I slowly made my way back home. All the excitement of going to the park had diminished and I told myself I would never go there again. I beat myself up for what happened that day and no matter how much I tried, I couldn't rid myself of the guilt I felt inside. It seemed no matter where I was; I always brought pain and suffering to myself.

It was hours before my siblings returned home, when they did they asked why I'd been crying but I couldn't tell them. I felt ashamed of being molested yet again, it had happened so many times I thought I might recognise the signs before it happened again so I was angry with myself for not being able to. Andrew was annoyed that I hadn't joined them at the park. He had carried Simon a long way without taking a break so he didn't speak to me for the rest of the day, but I saw that as nothing more than a blessing. I don't recall saying much at all during that day; I'd been traumatized by what had happened as I hadn't experienced being molested outside the home before. I had always felt reasonably safe on the streets but that tragic moment changed everything. I couldn't rid myself of the scrutiny written on that man's face, it seemed so much worse being molested by a stranger but as time passed and our struggle for survival went on, my ordeal seemed to become less significant. I became so nervous I had a tendency to expect the worst in all things and so was reluctant to go out. I remained indoors, where I couldn't be seen. This left Andrew and Lorraine free to roam the streets searching for food on their own. They found bits of mouldy cheese and rotten fruit in the dustbins at the back of the Co-op, which they shared with Simon and myself but it wasn't enough to take our hunger away.

The Co-op was ideally situated across from our house, so I was able to look through our bedroom window and watch out for them but I hadn't the courage to go and help them. For the first time ever Frank got annoyed with us. The stench around the bins began to affect the tenants in the flats above the shops and each in turn threatened to call the police. So this unnerved me all the more.

It was some time before I dared go to the park again. Instead, I chose to visit places that I'd remembered going to when Mother and Father had been at home. A place I felt safe was the 'Foxen Dam'. It was quite a distance from our house but it was the only area I knew that was isolated - where we could paddle and pick bluebells. We took a short cut through the estate, along many lanes and through thick woods; it seemed miles from where we lived but it was peaceful, almost desolate. Although on occasions we were startled by the loud shrill of birds echoing through the trees, we'd laugh so much that tears of joy rolled down our cheeks.

As a child, I knew very few places where I could escape to - this was a place where I felt free and totally out of reach. I was at peace there. It was the perfect place where I could reflect and forget everything that was bad; it was my haven! My paradise!

We paddled in shallow water, skimmed stones across the dam and picked bluebells by the armful. As the sun's rays glistened through the trees, the water rippled silently around the edges producing a magnificent range of colour. I gave sudden thought to the beautiful aroma that filled the air and triggered the only good memories I had of my childhood - when we walked through the woods as a family. I recall visiting the woods after church on Sundays with Mother and Father when they lived at home. Like other children, I was full of inno-cence and held all the love and happiness in the world but suddenly it had all changed and there I was - just a little girl, all alone.

I loved the beauty of bluebells. For me they held something special. The vibrant colours and their poignant scent gave me a strong sense of security, reminding me, taking me way back to the past – there had been good times! Most parents still visited the woods and paddled the dam alongside their children, taking along a picnic and walking their dogs just like we used to, but now we visited the woods alone, going only when other children were in school.

School was a thing of the past. I could remember going when we all lived together, but it seemed such a long time since I'd walked through the school gates. I never liked it much especially when Father left home,

I found it really tough. I had always found it difficult to interact so fights broke out between me and other children when they called me names and laughed at my clothing. Mother couldn't afford much, replacing our shoes and clothing was totally out of her reach so we had to make do. She tried mending clothing that was torn but she wasn't the best at needlework. Although she made an effort to keep our clothes clean, they were un-ironed and so discoloured they looked old and ragged. Our woollens had grown so out of shape we looked a pitiful sight. Mother told me many times, 'You should think yourself lucky,' and I did, but I still couldn't understand why it was me who had to wear the hand-me-downs. She didn't realise how difficult that was for me, yet I was repeatedly ridiculed because of it; even my siblings called me second - hand Rose.

I can never remember Mother having enough money. She rarely bought coal to keep us warm yet I remember her occasionally buying some to heat the hot water for our laundry - her budget was so tight our personal hygiene was often affected by it.

I remember her regularly bathing as she repeatedly reminded us "cleanliness is next to godliness" yet she considered our hygiene far less important than hers. I remember my hair being in a terrible mess, regularly matted, infested with head lice. I scratched like crazy and she'd chastise me for it, like it was my fault. I carried the foul smell of urine on my clothing through bed wetting and the strong odour of sexual abuse that had now become part of me. It was something I'd always lived with so hadn't realised how bad things were until my school friends began running away from me, telling me I stunk and refusing to sit next to me in class because of it.

My older siblings often passed comment, pushing me away when I got close to them. It seemed most of my family recognised that I had an unusually strong odour about me but gave no thought to question why.

I don't specifically recall the first time I was abused by my brother John, but I know it was very early on in my life. I recall times when he collected me from Chestnut Avenue Infant School, soon after I was admitted. My mood changed instantly when I walked up the drive to the school gates and saw him standing there. It was a sign no one was at home and I knew instantly he would be taking advantage of the situation by sexually abusing me once we arrived home. My laughter changed to a half-hearted smile knowing he was only there to hurt me. I was too young to hate, but I remember thinking I must have been the most horrible child in school. I felt troubled and uneasy and worried constantly about the pain he caused me. I didn't know that what he was doing was wrong, only that it was so painful, I cried all the way through it. He ordered me not to tell anyone about the things that he did to me and because I was too small to stop him it became part of my life.

His inflictions were worse than torture. He caused me so much pain performing acts of vaginal and anal intercourse, I cried at the thought I might die. The word 'no' didn't fit in to his vocabulary so when I screamed and called out for Mother, he showed no sympathy or remorse and insisted I would grow to like it – but I knew I wouldn't. My tears only seemed to add to his excitement and my continued wailing provoked the most unnatural response in him.

I'll never forget the day when Carol noticed blood on my pants as she undressed me ready for bed, she was in her teens and knew a little about womanly things so she knew something wasn't quite right. My stomach turned as she began to question why, but I was terrified to tell her how it had got there - for fear I was in the wrong. I sensed she already knew and I was upset by it. She told Mother she had a strong suspicion I was being molested and pointed out the blood but, it fell on deaf ears and nothing was pursued or changed.

He abused me at every given opportunity and created many situations where we were left alone in the house, even when it meant he had to take care of our younger siblings too. He showed no suspicion of his intentions and treated me as cruelly as the others so as not to raise concern.

There had been many times when he came close to being discovered by other members of the family, but he always seemed prepared for them. He moved fast when he heard voices and re-dressed quickly to make himself look innocent - even after causing me hours of pain and suffering. He staged an entirely different scene before anyone came in, regularly getting me in to trouble for being in places I shouldn't be, showing no remorse when I was being punished for being out of bed when I should have been in it and fast asleep.

I had never been entirely happy, not even when Father was still at home, but when he left, my life got worse. Being one of the youngest I had a lot to put up with. I had six older siblings each with a cruel streak, but John's cruelty outweighed everyone's. He made my life unbearable but I was too frightened to let anyone know.

I suffered regularly when my older brothers fought. They wrestled me to the ground, forcing my arms around my back then sat on me so my face was pressed hard to the floor. They were supposed to allow me to move when I cried 'submit' – it was a word we used for surrender, but when I cried and yelled 'submit' I was hurt even more. They couldn't bear to see me walk away unscathed as they found so much excitement in causing pain; they were thrilled by it.

I struggled when they restrained me but I wasn't strong enough to fight them off. Each of them had the strength of an ox and knew they could hurt me. I screamed and called them names but they laughed and joked about my weaknesses and none of my sisters volunteered to protect me, as they accepted the whole routine as fun. I hated wrestling, it was painful and distressing, and the results were always the same - I ended up covered in bruises and crying in pain while they stood there laughing at me. But I blamed John for what took place! He was the instigator of the wrestling and found as much pleasure in hurting my siblings as they found in hurting me. He encouraged violence amongst us all and jeered as we fought. For him it proved to be a magnificent pastime.

I remember suffering as a child many injuries through sibling rivalry and misconduct. I clearly recall David and Trevor causing me unnecessary pain through their constant rivalry as they argued and fought at the drop of a hat. David was much older and wiser than Trevor so had the upper hand every time. But Trevor had such a temper he found it hard to control his whim of picking up objects to throw at David. I remember the object Trevor chose one particular day was heavy and it flew through the air hitting our television screen with such force it exploded with a huge bang and left me screaming as thousands of tiny glass fragments shot through the air, piercing my skin as they embedded themselves into my body. I gave out such a scream it bought Mother crashing into our front room with panic written all over her face, the shock of seeing glass stuck to my face like porcupine's needles stuck to its back, brought out the worst in her and she began to scream a huge amount of abuse at my brothers then some more at Carol, for not watching me. Having ordered Carol to fetch Father she screamed some more until she was blue in the face.

I was hysterical and shook with fear yet in all the time she stood there looking at me, she hadn't thought to comfort me. Father was at our neighbour's house where he took refuge when things got tough and we got a little out of hand, so Mother didn't know what to do. My father had many weaknesses, the sight of blood being one of them. He found any injury distressing, but on this occasion he ran into our front room where I was standing and knelt down in front of me, pulled out the pieces of glass that had embedded themselves into my arms and legs then wiped my skin clean as the cuts began to bleed. I expected pain, but he was so gentle I only felt a small amount and cried just a little. My face hurt much more. I screamed as he pulled at the first piece of glass, it was obvious it was embedded far deeper than he thought and made the pain much worse, so being a man of warmth and feeling he wrapped me up in his overcoat and took me to the hospital.

Although I'd spent a lot of time in hospital I still feared them and cried all the way there. I was terrified, but the nurse on duty was able to put me at ease and removed every piece of glass with tenderness, leaving thread-like cuts that smarted severely when she covered them with antiseptic. A few hours later she sent me home smiling as she let me go.

By the time Father and I had arrived home our family had returned to normal, no one asked me how I was feeling and not a single word was mentioned about the injuries or my pain. I was left on a chair to recover and no more was said about it. It was generally the case when one got hurt. It wasn't important enough for anyone to be concerned as getting hurt was so frequent, it was taken in one's stride. It wasn't until I got older that I realised there had been so many accidents in and around our home, the family accepted it as the norm.

—∿—

CHAPTER 3

What It was Like to Go Hungry

In a family as large as ours, it was inevitable there would be favourites among us. Anne set the trend by favouring Lorraine, our baby girl, until Simon was born then all her attention went on him.

Julie followed suit by favouring Trevor, she clung to him like treacle on a spoon and tucked him under her wing. But when she went to boarding school he was lost without her so attached himself to David, who was far too old for Trevor and very much a loner, so kept himself to himself much of the time. He hated having Trevor around especially when he was with his own friends, a selected few chosen by David, who didn't take kindly to having Trevor for company so David began to hit him when Mother wasn't around. Poor Trevor spent much of his time crying, but still tagging along with David, begging to go with him; this caused a lot of trouble and fights broke out between them.

Carol had a soft spot for Andrew, the brother with the brightest crop of copper coloured hair. She loved him for the mass of freckles that covered his face and for those who didn't appreciate them the way she did, she spent most her time convincing them they where a sign of beauty and the best things since slice bread.

That left John who was the family bully, he was cruel and sadistic so didn't get on with anyone. He had spent much of his childhood away from home for committing arson when he was only seven, so grew up very different to the rest of us. He practiced a lot of wicked things, including intimidating our parents. None of us knew him really, not the real John, not even Mother and Father.

He got us all into a lot of trouble, constantly lying when he stole things and made us confess to things we hadn't done so that he could clear his own name and still be Mother's golden boy. No matter what anyone thought, he ruled the roost.

Me, I had my father and looked forward to seeing him when he came home after a hard day's work, selling logs. He had a lot of time for us, playing games we will never forget. He was the only one that showed any affection, making us feel really special. Always tired and out of breath, yet still made time to play with us before falling to sleep in his usual upright position on his chair - at the side of the kitchen fire. Occasionally there were times when Mother got really angry and paired me off with Carol while she tried to work. I wasn't one for mixing and already suffered a personality complex that influenced my behaviour. I was conscious of everything; I knew that Mother couldn't bear to have me around while Father was at home and Carol hated taking me out with her.

Carol was eight years my senior so wouldn't tolerate having me around if she didn't want me. She was clearly the most violent girl in our family so it was nothing to her to bully me, knowing I was the weaker child. I followed her around when she went out like Mother told me to but she only thumped me and insisted I went off on my own. I spent a lot of my time wandering the streets alone. Although there were 10 of us, I didn't seem to fit in anywhere.

It's not quite clear to me at what point Anne and Julie left home, but I know I was very young at the time and soon after, John found David part time work on Wards Farm. Andrew and Trevor went on doing their own thing. Lorraine was too young to leave the house and so stayed home with Mother. I'm sure Simon wasn't born at this stage as I have no memory of him at all during that time.

That left Carol who, at that stage of her life, really wanted to go out socialising, but unfortunately she got lumbered with me - I paid a heavy price. She taught me things I shouldn't have known at my age and showed me how to steal money from Beattie, a pensioner who lived in a bungalow not far from our house. Beattie was deaf, so I found it easy to steal from her especially when her carer wasn't there. Sometimes, I was clumsy and got caught but my fear of the police was far less than the fear I had of Carol, so it made little difference to me. The money I stole, I gave to Carol hoping it would please her and she'd stop hitting me. Once she had cigarettes and bottles of beer she seemed happier and tended to show me a little more respect than usual. I picked up a lot of her characteristics and learned the knack of stealing without making mistakes. I stole empty beer bottles for her from behind the West End pub where she knew she could return them for refunds, and then I would watch her spend the money in the off-license at the same pub.

Guinness and stout bottles were her favourites; she received a bigger refund on those. So it became a regular habit of ours. Her excuse for making me steal was that if I got caught it wouldn't be as bad for me as it would be for her. Being a small child and all, I was supposed to be able to get away with it. I believed her and took full responsibility when we did get caught but I wasn't so easily forgiven.

Eventually I became dissatisfied with the fact that she was taking every penny off me when I'd worked so hard to steal for her, so I refused to steal any more, but she got so angry she punched me in my mouth and tormented me in front of her friends. She was abusive and thought nothing of embarrassing me in front of people she knew. I was embarrassed about wetting the bed and had the most intense and unreasonable fear of men with disfigurements and cried uncontrollably at the awful things she said to me, so stealing the glass bottles was soon back on again.

I despised her for turning me into the ruthless little girl I became, but there was nothing I could do to change it. I don't recall telling Mother or Father about Beattie or the West End pub and I'm sure if I had it wouldn't have made much difference. They were aware of our dishonesty, but they simply had no control over it. During the times Anne was home from work, she and Carol argued over everything which made my life a little more bearable, they competed regularly against each other, which took Carol's attention away from me and I was left to ponder things over in my young brain. Anne led a full social life and constantly provoked Carol into jealousy so the friction between them began the minute Anne walked through the front door. Our parents had very little control over my older siblings so regardless of what was said, they couldn't stop the violence that took place between them.

During the weekends, Anne spent a tremendous amount of time cleaning the Pentecostal church, ensuring that the large displays of flowers that stood on the piano and in the windows around the church were fresh. She practiced for hours on their piano, so that she didn't make mistakes when she played during Sunday service. She was so involved in the church she seemed oblivious to everything that went on around her. Our parents' constant struggle to feed and clothe us seemed far less important to her once she had become a church member and I remember Mother telling her so. Although she knew how desperate they were, she still gave more support to the church than she did to them or us, her brothers and sisters. If they didn't attend church, they barely saw her.

I remember Mother sitting at our kitchen table, crying like I had seen her so many times before. She was wondering how to feed us and worried so much, she could barely hold her head up. She had already suffered a breakdown and was heading for another but even so it seemed Anne put her friends before her family. Carol seemed to have a better understanding of the family's situation so taking a cloth sack from Father's tool shed, she lead David, Trevor and myself to a large potato field at the edge of the park and made us dig through the earth searching for potatoes and turnips to feed ourselves with. We dug deep into the soil with our bare hands pulling out enough potatoes and turnips to fill the sack. When it was full, Carol gathered the top of the sack together and threw it over her shoulder and carried it home. Mother accepted it with gratitude but showed a little concern, when she begged us never to steal again. She was terrified of us getting caught, but she knew as well as we did, if we were hungry, we'd steal and there was nothing much she could do about it.

After drying her eyes, she looked around and tried to look pleasant. I have never forgotten the look of relief that swept over her face that night as she hastily prepared mashed potato and turnip for our suppers. It was the only meal we'd had for weeks. The rest of the time, we ate what we could scrounge. When Anne found out what we had eaten she and Carol fought most of the night. Anne knew stealing was wrong and no amount of hunger would have changed her thoughts on that, but Carol understood things differently, reminding Anne it wasn't her that was suffering. She pointed out how over-weight she was in comparison to us little ones and reminded her of the hot meal she had just eaten at her boyfriend's home and the tea she had shared with her church friends, whilst we ate nothing. Carol spoke of all the times she had bought sweets for herself, while Mother struggled to earn enough money to buy a loaf of bread to feed us with. Anne didn't know what it was like to go hungry, she was one of the lucky ones who had everything going for her. She was different to us and had a lot of good ways, but she couldn't help putting her own needs before everyone else's.

Sometimes, she brought coloured ribbons for our hair and white plastic sandals for Whit Sunday and arranged for us to go to Tarentum Gardens every year with the church. She was given bonnets and clothes by the family she worked for; but for everything she did, we still went hungry.

Carol resented Anne for having a better life than we had. It was apparent that when she was a child she had been spoiled by both sets of grandparents and so had no idea what we were going through. She had had everything lavished upon her, including private tuition to teach her to play the piano which resulted in her playing fluently yet, she failed to pursue it. Grandma was still alive when she was a little girl and helped Mother make Anne some wonderful clothes.

We had photographs of her pushing a doll's pram and playing with the most enchanting dolls' house I could only dream about, the flouncy lace dresses she wore were dotted with ribbons and bows, the photos showed her hair had been neatly set in ringlets and dangled at each side of her face. She wore pure white socks trimmed with lace and beautiful leather shoes neatly tied with bows, something I hadn't a hope of experiencing. My only footwear had been my white plastic sandals that I wore in summer and winter alike. Anne's photographs meant everything to me; they were just like the pictures I had seen of Susan and Mary in the Ladybird books I discovered in school. She looked beautiful with pretty white petticoats and clean white socks and a beautiful velvet dress to top the lot, like a fairy on a Christmas tree - too good to be real.

I was never able to understand why my parents' lives and ours had changed so much over the years, but I knew they had become very poor with every day a struggle. Mother had many different jobs trying to make ends meet but earned only a pittance. Father was fifteen years her senior and suffered from emphysema, so found it difficult to work. He tried selling logs when he felt well enough but the money he earned was nowhere near enough to look after all our needs. There had been times when I saw him in so much pain he could barely move but Mother nursed him every day helping him, aiding his recovery; as she did for all of us when we were ill. Sometimes I secretly cried for my parents, often praying for Mother to have more strength and for God to make Father well again, I loved them so much, I was heartbroken to see them in so much pain.

Mother brought home so little money that substantial meals were few and far between, what we had was unusual and cost very little yet still took a large percent of Mother's wages. I ate sugar on dry bread and occasionally ketchup on bread and butter. I ate everything she put in front of me and never complained. Bread was the largest part of our diet because it was cheap and something Mother could afford and at least guaranteed us a meal. I recall her counting the slices in a loaf making sure it had the usual twenty-three slices she needed, occasionally making me take it back to the Co-op to ask Frank to change it if there weren't. I was barely six years old at this time but was still embarrassed when I had to ask him to count the slices before I dared take the loaf home to her. Frank always obliged as he had experienced Mother's anger before and was only too pleased to help. He knew there were only twelve of us including my parents, but considering Gyp and Kim, our dogs, we needed the extra two slices so they didn't go without, so he did everything in his power to ensure I had a twenty-three sliced loaf to go home with.

Sometimes Mother had a little extra money in her wage packet and was able to buy a tin of soup and some potatoes, the soup was watered down with a double quantity of water and it helped to feed all of us. H.P sauce was my father's favourite, he'd spread it sparingly on bread and butter then hide the bottle on the top shelf in the pantry so we couldn't get at it. But when Mother was really short of money and could only afford bread and butter my brothers complained it wasn't enough. I remember how Mother would remind them it was "best butter, not Stork". Being so young, that statement had no significance for me, but it seemed to work wonders with my brothers - as they howled with laughter.

Carol left school at the age of fourteen, found a job fairly quickly and began to enjoy independence. She worked full time in a factory close to our home and was really excited when she received her first wage packet, but Mother stood waiting for her to return home that Friday night and took all her wages from her. It was to help feed everyone in the house and she promised faithfully to pay her back, but Carol found it hard to understand why she should contribute to the upkeep of the household when none of the others did. I remember them shouting and screaming as the wage packets where torn apart and Carol crying every Friday night just hoping her tears might help change Mother's mind, but desperation forced Mother to act and she took everything, leaving Carol with nothing.

Carol's wages compensated for the wages John wouldn't give up, he never contributed towards his own keep and made it clear he wouldn't contribute towards anyone else's. He earned far more than Carol but spent every penny on himself, never considering anyone. Mother was far too frightened to ask him for anything and Father too ill to persuade him, he ruled through his violence. He still ate the food Mother bought but cared nothing about us little ones going without. Everyone else who lived at home during that time was under working age.

Anne gave money to Mother if she was staying at home for the weekend but with an extra mouth to feed, it didn't last long. Julie had now left home for good and was living with a family of fairground people so didn't come back home to live. She occasionally visited during summer and again on Christmas Eve with her boyfriend Chris, but come Boxing Day she returned to her lodgings. She rarely came home once she'd found work on the fairground, and apart from the occasional visit, we hardly saw her.

—⁂—

≈ CHAPTER 4 ≈

Our Last Christmas

I remember Christmas 1966 as being a happier time. It was a rare occasion when all the family pulled together making Christmas really special. Mother went to town shopping with Father, Anne and Carol, each on a different day coming home laden with all sorts of goodies and extra special things. They bought biscuits, nuts and cake, fruit and crackers and a small sprig of mistletoe to add to the Christmas cheer. I remember all our excitement, as I stood in the kitchen alongside Trevor, Andrew and Lorraine who where giving out screams of delight when each member of our family emptied the contents of their bags onto the kitchen table. The amount of food was unbelievable! Our younger siblings became so giddy they overflowed with excitement. Father surprised us all and brought us each a small piece of liquorice root when it was his turn, he knew it was a favourite of ours and said it would do us good.

We were a large family so it took Mother several trips to town on the bus before she was satisfied we had enough food to last the whole of the holiday. All our family came together, Mother and Carol baked on Christmas Eve, making the stocks of mince pies and jam tarts and Father roasted chestnuts on the open fire before we went to bed. I was so excited I couldn't sleep. Lying awake for hours I listened for St Nick but before I knew it, I was fast asleep and morning was upon me. I raced downstairs searching for the usual sack of toys I'd been accustomed to receiving each year and to my delight our front room had once again been decorated with paper garlands, lanterns and full of Christmas cheer.

The Christmas tree stood on the wooden table in the corner of the room. Once again, it had been dressed with silver tinsel and pretty novelty lights that gave our room a nice warm glow, making it feel really special. The fire still burning a few red coals flickered shadows around the flowered papered walls. A large bucket of coal placed at the side of the hearth ready for the rest of the day, and there in front of our settee stood four modest bags of toys labeled Trevor, Molly, Andrew, and Lorraine. It had been the same routine every year for as long as I could remember and yet, my heart still filled with joy and pounded with excitement as I entered our front room.

It was still dark outside, but a thick layer of snow brightened the sky. It had been snowing for a few days and gave rooftops and tips of the trees a white frosted glow as the last few flakes fell slowly from the sky - the picture from our front room window gave me a feeling of warmth and contentment. There was something about the night sky carrying the snow that I loved. It could have been the huge flakes that fell and rested on our windows for a second, then, disappeared from view or the unspoiled snow getting ever deeper on our garden like the icing on our Christmas cake, no prints or marks to spoil it; a blanket of perfection in a small child's life.

That year we all had good meals and we ate right through Christmas day to the New Year. But once Anne returned to work and Julie to her lodgings, Carol and John argued over the scraps that were left and "good will to all men" was soon forgotten. It was so difficult to face reality after everything had been so perfect, but with a family like ours it was hard to believe Christmas survived as well as it did.

Looking back at that final Christmas, I feel sure my parents knew it was the end of the road for them. It was the last Christmas we spent together and proved to be the beginning of our family breakup.

—⁓—

~ CHAPTER 5 ~

God Give Me Strength

As another Year passed, Mother cleaned the house and gave us our occasional bath always using the remainder of the coal to heat the water. Her approach to that New Year had been different to what it had been like on previous years, it seemed she was prepared to start the year by turning over a new leaf and made every effort to get us back to school.

She had already received numerous threats from the school board about our non-attendance and hadn't many chances left. Our clothes had already been washed and put aside for the new term but as usual the thought of returning to school gave me a dreadful feeling of anxiety, I felt sick to my stomach. I had lost so much time at school I couldn't read, write, count or spell. The fear of going back to receive countless reminders of how slow and stupid I was from the teacher I knew as Miss Chalmers caused me to loath her even more than I did already. I didn't want to face the constant ridicule from her or my classmates so I made up all kinds of excuses as to why I shouldn't go. Mother didn't listen, she had made up her mind and tried hard to maintain a regular routine of sending me to school without any interruptions. I remember she placed us in the bath three at a time, scrubbed us all down with Fairy and carbolic, and tried her best to look cheerful, but her efforts always seemed to be in vain.

Every now and again I saw her pick up her apron to wipe a tear from the corner of her eye, trying to smile - she casually passed it off as something in her eye. I left for school first thing Monday morning with my hands stuffed into my coat pockets and my chin resting on my chest wishing I was anywhere but on my way to school.

Her routine ran well for a while but it wasn't long before I was back roaming the streets on the days I should have been at school, picking up sweets and pieces of gum that had been trodden so firmly into the ground I had to spend time scraping it up, just to satisfy my hunger pangs, while I was playing truant.

I played around shop doorways, occasionally stealing a twist of barley sugar, passing time while other children where in school, but Mother found out and when I got home she grabbed me by the hair and bawled me out while giving me a quick slap about the head before sending me to bed, but I was used to violence so it had very little effect on me. After the beatings I'd suffered from John and Carol; that was nothing.

She had been sending me to school for weeks but I spent most of my time roaming the streets and playing around in the piglets' pen opposite Nightingale's shop. I hadn't been attending school at all, but up until that day no one seemed to care. She never asked why I wouldn't go and eventually she just palmed me off with my older brother David, but at times even he didn't go

After weeks of not attending everything had returned to normal, the stench on my clothes was enough to turn anyone's stomach and the untidy mess of my hair said it all. I hated school and tried my best not to attend but when she did eventually get me there, I generally got picked on. For me it was a place of persecution and I suffered at the hands of other children through my parents' hardship and neglect. I was about seven years old when I began taking notice of the state of my dress, previously I had been ignorant to the fact I had caused offence to those who came close to me but by the time I was eight I felt too ashamed to go near anyone. Mother didn't seem to care. When she dressed me for school she didn't acknowledge the terrible smell about me, it seemed natural for her to dress me in the same unwashed clothing that I had worn day in day out, week after week and even dismissed the fact, I rarely wore pants. I have never forgotten the true anguish I felt when I was regularly told by my classmates that I stank of pee and as an afterthought they would add; or something, with a puzzled look upon their face. Mother had no qualms about sending me to school in odd socks or the dress I had slept in but I cried at the thought of wearing it especially when I'd wet the bed and my own odour seemingly became more apparent. She often angrily mumbled her usual speech of not being able to afford the things we wanted and regularly pointed out how much she paid for clothing, just to enable me to go to school, but I knew that wasn't true.I can only ever remember large bags of second-hand clothing being delivered to our house from the children's welfare department; most of my clothing came from them.

My schooldays were very unhappy. When I was old enough to be admitted to the junior school on School Lane, I felt proud at the thought of attending a new school, but as time went by the children worked out which family I was from and then I became a target for constant bullying. The boys who knew of our family physically attacked me every night as I left school to walk home. I remember I was chased and beaten by a boy named John Riley, he was bold, forceful and the ring leader of a large gang. He had a family of brothers and sisters larger than ours, who knew mine very well and it soon became apparent that both our families had been rivals for some time. I hadn't met any of them up to meeting him, but instantly took a dislike to them. It was impossible for me to seek refuge or sympathy from my older siblings, they were strong and fought their own battles on the streets like barbarians, so my nervous disposition didn't go down well with any of them and they generally laughed at me for being weak.

The beatings and constant ridicule I suffered from John Riley went on for months and I only decided to tell the teacher when I became too frightened to leave the school. But the teacher's reprimand made no difference to him and things only got worse when he realised I had informed on him. A few days later he began to strip thin branches from trees and whip me around my bare legs using his full force to beat me, until I was heavily marked. He used his full force to lash the sticks around my head often causing bruising to my face and neck. I didn't know what was worse; the sticks or his fists. Whether he used his fists or sticks he was vicious and as much as I would have liked to have got my own back on him, I knew he was stronger than me, so I wouldn't even try. I didn't cry much, I was bred to be a tough little girl. Because of him, I became an outcast and began to really hate that school. His bright ginger hair made him stand out from a crowd so I hated that too. I tried to keep my distance from him but, once I was outside school, he made a run for me and caught me every time. Eventually I figured, if I ran fast enough I could get out of the school gates before anyone else and be on my way home, well before he came through the school gates, but on the days we took P.E. it didn't always work. His ginger hair helped me to recognise him amongst the crowd of other children, although I tried not to look back as the very sight of him terrified me.

I spent a lot of my childhood heartbroken and feeling miserable, desperately trying to get over everything that made me unhappy, wishing I could grow up faster and praying for things to change, hoping my life would get better. I made wishes that I might grow tall and age much faster. All I wanted was for someone to love me. I even remember the times when I asked my best friend if I could go and live with her, thinking I could run away from everything that was harmful, but my life remained the same no matter what I wished for.

I lived my life with poverty and hunger. If it had been just those two things maybe it would not have been so bad, but I hated the abuse from my brother. The more he took from me, the more he wanted. I hated the times when he disturbed my sleep by rubbing my vagina until it was sore. He did the most unnatural things - forcing his head between my thighs purposely to lick the inside of my vagina and poked his fingers inside, until I squirmed with pain, then mount me like a horse as he pulled my legs apart and forced his fully erected penis inside me. I cried and called for Mother but his first reaction was to cover my mouth with his hand firmly applying pressure before I was heard, and the tears I'd been holding back for so long streamed down my face covering his hands as I unwillingly gave in to him. The fact my younger siblings were in the same room, lying at the side of me did not deter him and it seemed until they began to stir he felt quite at ease having sex with me while they were present.

It was only when they stirred and sat up in bed oblivious to what was going on around them he'd grab hold of me to carry me through to the bathroom, like he had done so many times before. I trembled from head to foot as he roughly knocked me against each door frame as he rushed me through to the bathroom and placed me on the floor with the rest of the rubbish that had been left there. Kneeling in front of me, he forced my legs apart to match his own then fell back onto his heels bringing his height down to mine, enabling him to insert his penis in between my thighs without a struggle, moving me back and forth he ordered me to hold on to him while he raped me. It was a terrifying moment when he suddenly turned me away from him and guided me over the edge of the bath so my bottom was in full view, almost facing him. Pulling the cheeks of my bottom apart he furiously poked his tongue in and out of my anus. The pain of that alone was so unbearable I began to squirm begging him to stop, trying my damndest to pull away from his clutches so I could stand upright. But he got so angry he pushed me back with such force my head sprung forward and hit the bottom of the bath with a bang. He was never satisfied until he'd hurt me.

He held me down so he could force his fingers as far up inside my anal passage as he could, muttering my name, he relished the thought of hurting me. He tried many times to force his penis into my anus before he eventually succeeded but, when he did I screamed so loud his hand shot from my mouth and my screams could be heard all over the house. Carol came to my aid but, with practice John convinced her I was just messing around and said he'd deal with me and put me back into bed.

It was easy for her to believe him, he had been abusing me for so long the character he had given me fitted in well with the kind of person she thought I was. But underneath that tough exterior was a dainty little girl desperately trying to get away from the man that abused her. When he finally agreed to let me go I tried to leave the bathroom as quickly as I could but it seemed he couldn't let me go without attempting one more orgasm and he'd yank me away from the door by my arm, smirking as he stopped me from leaving. Raising one leg he'd place his foot onto the edge of the bath and grab hold of my hair pushing my face towards his penis. He had shown me lots of times how to perform oral sex so I did it almost naturally hoping to get it over and done with as quickly as I could, just to get out of his way.

As he slowly caressed his own penis I couldn't help feeling sick as the strong smell of sperm waft up my noise. He trembled as I began to heave, my feeling nauseous excited him and he grabbed my head with both hands as he forced his fully erect penis into my mouth and thrust violently, then with all the rigidity in his body, he ejaculated into my mouth sending ripples of sperm to the back of my throat, before forcing me to swallow.

Although he had been molesting me for years I still bled during each attack and began to realise it had become part of the excitement for him, he always inspected my vagina after each sexual performance and wiped away any sperm that trickled down my legs. If I bled too profusely he stayed with me in the bathroom until he was sure the bleeding had stopped, trying to convince me that he cared for me, but because he hurt me I knew that he didn't.

When the time came and I was finally asked by police officers how many times he had done this to me, I couldn't say and the sad thing about it is, I couldn't even now. It had happened so many times and so often I thought it was all part of growing up, I even thought it was something that happened to every child. The only thing I couldn't understand was why it was so painful. When I was asked to think back to when it first began, I couldn't ever remember not doing it, it had been happening to me from as far back as I could remember, way before my first day at the infant school; I believe it had been happening all my life. I was almost six years old when Carol finally bought it to light. She told Father of her suspicions and explained how John locked me in the bathroom with him for hours and gave her reasons for suspecting he was sexually abusing me. He was a good Father and reported it to the police straight away and I was removed from home immediately.

I was questioned in the police station for some time but didn't realise how serious it was until the police arrested John that same afternoon. Spending all day in the presence of police officers scared me. I wondered what I had done wrong. I was all alone. Mother was defending John so she wasn't allowed to accompany me. I recalled my last few days and tried to describe as much as I could but couldn't bring myself to tell them everything. I didn't understand which parts of it was wrong and the fear and embarrassment restricted the amount of information I could give, but I made a statement to the best of my ability not knowing which parts were most important. I ran through it as quickly as I could just to stop the police from badgering me, then I was taken to a local clinic where I was stripped and lay naked while I waited to be examined.

When I was finally allowed home I trembled and tried to understand why Mother was so angry with me, the fact she blamed me was horrible. She couldn't look me in the eye and I knew then, she hated me - without her even saying so.

I didn't see John again for three whole years. After going to court he was found guilty of several charges and went to prison to serve a four year sentence. Not understanding the rights and wrongs of child abuse, I wasn't really sure why he'd been sent away but there was no one more pleased than I, when I found out he wasn't coming home. Mother punished me for John being sent away. I suffered a lot of unhappy moments and although I was only six years old I became much older in my thinking and felt terribly ashamed and somewhat responsible for what had happened. I asked myself, as I still do now, when there were four more sisters, why did he have to choose me? I was the most plain, fragile little thing amongst all our family.

I had dark bobbed hair, as had 90 percent of children in those days, and looked no different to many others that attended my school and yet for some reason, he chose to make my life insufferable. There had been many times when I had wished so hard that I could die, I felt ashamed for having no reason for living. The acute pain, extreme pressure and complete secrecy had become such a burden, it was too much for me to handle. I lacked the intellect to understand John's reasons for keeping it all quiet but, I thanked God it was now in the open. The pain of keeping so much of my life to myself for so long; had made my life unbearable. I feared him when I was with him and still feared him when I wasn't. I remembered the days when I had deliberately wandered around the streets where I lived, trying desperately to delay the frequency of attacks he made upon me.

When no one was in our house, they happened more frequently and lasted far longer. He knew that I tried to avoid him, even when it meant being out of our house in the cold, without food and water. I can't remember how old I was when I began to hate my family, but it was way before it was brought to Father's attention. I hated them for having a life outside our home and for leaving me in the house unattended, but most of all I hated them for not seeing through him. My life had been hell while everyone around me had been living theirs as if I didn't exist. No one ever asked what I had been doing all day or whether I had attended school. No one ever wondered where I was when he had me locked up in the bathroom for hours and no one gave a damn while I was being hurt. I still now regularly ask myself, if it hadn't have been for Carol's observation, what kind of a person would I be today?

When I was finally free of him I recall things around our house being much different. Mother still didn't pay much attention to me and Father left home following a violent argument which left me pretty much on my own. Anne came home less frequently and we were assigned to a social worker; for the first time in my life I saw a light at the end of the tunnel.

Miss Woodward, our social worker, was kind to me and my siblings, often taking us out to parks where we mixed with other children. Although I tried hard not to be envious of other children and their lives I admired other girls of my age; I took particular note of their fine clothes and shoes that I'd give my all for and found myself wishing I was one of them. I loved it when we drove down to Whittington Park, the children were friendly and because no one knew us, we were accepted more readily than we'd ever been. I felt different there. As we drove through our estate and headed towards Chesterfield my heart began to pound and I'd slowly shuffle myself comfortable on the cold leather seats of her green Morris Traveller, my mind closed down and I began to relax. The feeling of being with someone who cared was more than I could bear, as I sat back I fell silent and almost cried as I realised Miss Woodward was probably the closest thing to a dream Mother I was going to get. I became so fond of her, even when she only called to visit, I insisted on sitting with her in the car before she left. She was the nicest person I had ever met and I loved seeing her. Mother never liked her, especially when she insisted on asking questions, and hated her looking around our house. But I myself found life at home more bearable. Although I didn't know what her job entailed I noticed Mother kept more of a routine while she was visiting. I remember sometimes she made such a fuss about her coming, Miss Woodward became nervous and would make alternative arrangements hoping Mother would be in a better frame of mind the next time she visited but nevertheless the visits continued.

I'd seen Mother pick up pans in a fit of temper and throw them at social workers when they had visited our house before, especially when they asked questions she had no intention of answering, giving them the impression she had a lot to hide. So, when Miss Woodward called, Mother saw it as an invasion of her privacy and became angry, throwing all her weight around encouraging her to leave. This was solely intended to frighten Miss Woodward hoping she'd stay away from the house. Sometimes I feared Mother as much as I did John and found myself wishing she was more like other mothers I had seen. She didn't co-operate with anyone, especially the local authorities. She knew she couldn't always do things the right way but hated the thought of being harassed and so hid behind closed doors, determined not to be victimised for it. She had let things get out of control but was too proud to accept any help from the welfare. Under no circumstances would she ever admit failure, although she and my father had both got to the stage where their own relationship had broken down, and they agreed to separate. Neither of them had considered how life would be for the one who was left with seven young children and a home to look after.

When Father packed his belongings and left, things got much worse. Mother had very little money to buy food and clothes and found it a struggle to pay the rent. She had relied on Father so much and she found when he left she was in a worse state than she had ever been before, so was forced into taking yet another job just to make ends meet. It wasn't long before she realised that with a family the size of ours, no amount of money ever seemed enough and she struggled to keep the roof above our heads. She couldn't afford to pay off her creditors to whom she owed money and regularly turned them away from the door. She owed Peter the door-to-door salesman lots of money for sheets and items of clothing she purchased for herself and my older siblings when

Father still lived at home, but it was typical of her to blame the poor quality of his merchandise when she couldn't keep up the payments, resulting in terrible rows that frightened us all. When she realised Father wasn't coming back she began to lose interest in her family and her home and began going out until the early hours of the morning. She was drinking and occasionally came in drunk until eventually she met with a friend whom she had known for some time and brought him back to our house. I had never seen him before, he was small and thin, around the same size as an eight – year - old child and not much taller than me at that time. He had a limp and seemed to walk to one side. I distinctly remember my siblings and I, laughing and sniggering behind his back – but underneath all the joviality I couldn't help feeling embarrassed and wondered why Mother didn't feel the same. I asked him all kinds of questions referring to his height but he told me plain and simply; he was born that way. I didn't resent him as we had had so many male visitors to our house in the recent past I was used to new faces and didn't understand what relationship he held with Mother, if any at all. Eventually I took it for granted that Joe had taken Father's place and seemed to accept him more readily than I should have.

But when Mother started spending more time with him than she did with us, I began to hate him for taking her away from us. He lived a good half-hour's walk away from our house in a small touring caravan on spare ground, right on the edge of our estate but, it didn't seem to make any difference to her, she still stayed with him leaving Carol and myself to care for our siblings. Carol then took the opportunity to stay at her boyfriend's house all night while David and Trevor worked until late on Ward's Farm, where John had worked before he went to prison. I was left at home caring for Andrew, Lorraine and baby brother Simon who was only a little older than one year.

I hated being left with my younger siblings, they were always hungry and cried continually for Mother and because I was frightened I cried too. When I got sad and lonely, I walked them all up to Ward's Farm to see David and Trevor but at times it was all in vain and even on the rare occasions that we managed to find them, I would receive the harshest telling off I'd ever had and be sent back home immediately. David got angry and called me 'stupid' for dragging the little ones up to the farm but he knew just as well as I did, come a few days later I'd be up there again dragging my siblings behind me. He was always telling me off for doing what I thought was right. Concerned with my conduct he explained how dangerous it was for us to roam the lanes at night because of the farm machinery using them, but eventually he'd calm down and then show me the safest way home. I hated leaving David at the farm, he was my only security and I felt safe with him so I cried all the way back home. I carried Simon in my arms as he slept but I struggled with the other two, I was tired and all I wanted to do was sleep. I was frightened and felt so unloved, I really hated my family for leaving me feeling this way. I was cold and lonely, the sun had gone down and the lanes were dark, I feared every sound and shadow that we came across. I walked quietly but quickly, moving closer to my younger siblings just to give myself the feeling of security, tired and heartbroken I struggled, but eventually we made it home.

When David and Trevor came home they apologised for telling me off then bribed me with a huge duck egg if I cooked them some chips. It was usual for them to come home well after midnight feeling exhausted from the heavy duties and the long hours they worked. I was always asleep in bed by the time they came home but, I was so hungry just the thought of a trickling egg yolk persuaded me to get up – and after all I was the one who could peel all the potatoes in the short time it took them to peel just one. I would stand in our kitchen for hours cooking piles of chips, but when I had done I was allowed to feast on the best meal I'd had all day.

Mother didn't come home from Joe's very often but when she did she found David and Trevor sprawled out on the kitchen floor, fast asleep. She'd send them to bed and I'd hear them making their way upstairs, struggling to climb into their bunk beds. It had started to get light and had turned so cold even I was shivering underneath my blankets. A couple of hours later they'd be up, out of bed and off to the farm again without so much as a sigh. They went to work early, giving themselves the opportunity to steal duck eggs and potatoes without anyone seeing them. When the farmer was busy they'd hide stuff around the farm then collect it before coming home at night. Although the farmer seemed to think he paid them well, they received very little pay for the work they did, and had it not been for the food they stole and what I rummaged from the bins our family would never have survived.

I remember the days seemed to last much longer once Mother had returned to Joe's and my brothers were at the farm. Although David usually made sure we had a shilling in the gas meter, enabling me to cook their suppers he didn't always have enough to put one in the electricity meter. Many times I was left caring for my younger siblings in the dark and cold feeling hungry, walking the streets begging door to door for a shilling for the electricity meter. I'd been to the same doors that many times our neighbours began to refuse me further hand-outs. Because I was getting older I was often frowned upon and turned away with a large mouthful of abuse. At eight years old I was expected to walk away politely then say "thank-you" but I just told them to fuck off and ran like hell – back home to cook by candlelight. At times I'd fumble my way around the kitchen keeping my eyes firmly closed so the dark didn't frighten me. When I was forced to open them I barely managed to see the faint glow of light given out from the burning gas flame on our cooker and hadn't always managed to cook successfully as there were huge smoke rings on the ceiling where I'd previously set the chip pan on fire. I remember setting our pans on fire more than once but even so none of my older siblings offered to take my place or cook for me. It was easy for them to keep telling me to pay attention and watch what I was doing while they sat back judging me, but it wasn't easy doing all the work when I was so tired and still so very young.

Occasionally, Carol came back to spend a few nights at home but she'd get angry and throw stuff around when she couldn't find anything to eat and forced me to go begging when there was no gas or electricity. It didn't matter what time of night it was she still insisted that I went to ask neighbours for money and food on the pretence I'd be returning it the day after. I cried so I didn't have to go but she insisted, no matter what I did. I felt embarrassed returning to the neighbours I had cursed and sworn at the night before, but sometimes they would be kind and offer me something, knowing I was desperate. But at other times I was repeatedly sent away from their doors. They were angry at me getting them out of bed, they called me names for being inconsiderate but Carol never allowed me to take 'no' for an answer so I learned to be insistent. After slapping me around and kicking me half way around the streets, she sent me begging again and again to houses I had never been to, never allowing me to go home empty handed. Once she'd obtained gas and electricity at our neighbour's expense, she took Andrew and me to steal vegetables from the nearby fields while Lorraine and Simon slept soundly in their beds. Lorraine was only four and Simon was still a baby, but Carol didn't seem to think, when she made a decision she carried it out, no matter what the circumstances were.

When we arrived home with the vegetables, she forced me to peel lots of large potatoes while she cut up a turnip which she cooked and mashed together for our suppers. I wasn't really sure it was worth the wait or the physical abuse but it seemed to go down well and I slept a whole lot better for having a full stomach so I didn't complain.

I recall lorries loaded with cans of food and covered with green tarpaulin sheets parked in the close near our house from which David and Trevor stole baked beans and other canned foods. It fed us for days and as they were often there, we had a regular supply of the foods we really enjoyed. Unfortunately it didn't last forever so we had no alternative but to revert back to the basic potato and turnip that grew in the fields. We stole anything that was edible – it was the way we survived.

Mother visited our house once a week, usually on Fridays when Carol pleaded with her to stay home. But arguments broke out between them over lots of issues, especially money and food, so sometimes I was glad that she didn't stay. Mother just didn't seem to understand how important it was for her to stay and take care of us; she left us all alone to struggle on. My siblings screamed and the memory of that still echoes through my mind as I recall their tears falling freely down their cheeks as they hung on to Mother's coat begging her to stay, she pulled away kissing us on our cheeks before she waved goodbye. It was as though she was just going shopping, but I knew different. Every Friday she gave each of us a penny then walked away from us without a measure of guilt or concern, waving and calling "see you soon," like it was the most natural thing in the world.

She never mentioned school or anything else until Carol gave her a letter from the children's welfare department, then she stayed home. Mother, Carol and I cleaned our house from top to bottom sweeping and scrubbing floors with bleach and disinfectant, washing all the dirty clothes and bedding that had been stored under the sink for weeks and buying enough food to last until Miss Woodward had been. Of course it was important to impress the children's welfare and Mother wanted them to think she was coping well, but once they had been and gone, she left us again until the next time. It must have been months before my younger siblings and I realised that Mother was only living on Fenshaw Lane, a few miles away in Joe's caravan. My first reaction was to go up and see her but Joe hadn't been very nice to me so I was a little apprehensive, I knew he wouldn't like me around his caravan. Previously I had stolen his Jap desert and liquorice comfit sweets that were wrapped in two white paper bags and refused to admit to it even though I faced another beating. I was hungry and would have eaten anything. Mother was lucky she had gotten much larger than she was before and fared pretty well since she had left us to fend for ourselves.

Joe had never been married so didn't have any children of his own so at times I think he resented us. I was right in the assumption he wouldn't like me in his caravan. When I eventually felt brave enough to go up there none of us were made welcome and we were sent back home with a flea in our ear. We were told never to visit again unless we were invited, of course we never were. We saw Mother only when she came home for a visit but knowing where she was made all the difference. I felt a lot happier knowing she was still around, although I wasn't allowed to go and see her. The period of time between each of her visits to our home got longer and Fenshaw Lane seemed to get further and further away. I cried when I passed the lane where she now lived but that still wasn't enough to force me into changing the direction in which I was going. She had made herself a stranger so I tended to think of her as such. Andrew and Lorraine couldn't understand why I dragged them away from that area when they knew she was there. But she had made it clear to me that she wasn't pleased on previous occasions when I took them to see her so I chose to avoid her at all costs, hoping one day she would return to us.

Mother had this strange notion that visiting once a week and buying food for a day gave us the will to live the other six days without. By now I was still no more than eight years old, but God gave me enough strength and ability to use my skills to obtain food, doing whatever I could to maintain Andrew, Lorraine and Simon and some semblance of a family.

It has been over forty years now and in all that time I had seen my stealing as a sin. But as I sit here at my desk glancing over the photographs of my children and my children's children I realise God couldn't have seen it that way, so I thank him for the gift of life and for his continuing guidance.

Unfortunately my ability to care for my three younger siblings and myself, didn't stretch to washing our clothes so for months we wore the same clothes, changing only if it rained and we got wet. Then we wore other dirty clothing that we had worn before and usually carried the foul smell of urine. Andrew wore dresses that belonged to Lorraine and I, as there were no trousers to fit him. This was one of the few times we all raised a smile. He looked quite funny, yet I thought his red wavy hair and freckles made him look so much prettier than me and Lorraine.

As time passed we began to see Mother even less than once a week. We almost accepted we may never see her again as the visits she made became so few and far between. My younger siblings didn't cry for her like they had done in the past and the little time I spent thinking about her I did without shedding a single tear. Everyone above the age of fourteen had now abandoned us. David had become our eldest sibling that I relied upon, but he worked on the farm from morning until night, so I never saw him until well after midnight, when he woke me from my sleep to cook their suppers.

I took advantage of every situation, when they lay on the kitchen floor, exhausted and falling to sleep, I peeled their potatoes twice as thick so I was able to cook my younger siblings and myself a meal the day after – when I was able to scrape the skin from the peelings and fry them for us to eat. Very often this would be the only meal my younger siblings had had for days. At that stage no one ever asked if our younger siblings had eaten during the day so, if it hadn't been for me, they wouldn't have eaten at all. The instinct of survival was so strong anything stolen at night was usually eaten that night, none of us showed any sense of guilt while we were hungry and nobody but I ever thought about feeding the younger ones.

When the weather turned cold and winter set in, food became scarce and David and Trevor began to hide the food they stole. I searched the house every day looking for it but it wasn't very often I found any. On the rare occasions I did, they punched and kicked me for taking the only meal they could have had if I hadn't eaten it first.

There came a time when the punching and kicking no longer carried weight, I had become so used to them losing their temper with me I almost expected it. Although I cried following their beatings, it still didn't hurt as much as the pain in my stomach when I hadn't eaten. As the dark nights drew closer and it got cold we stole coal from our neighbours' coal sheds to keep warm. We waited until after midnight, as there was less chance of being caught and by that time David and Trevor had returned from the farm and all our neighbours were in bed. We took it in turns to keep a lookout while we filled cloth sacks that we had rummaged from the stuff left in Father's tool sheds. I couldn't carry much so Andrew came to help but even then, we only half filled the sacks. David and Trevor managed to steal full sacks but they wouldn't do it until they had eaten. Sometimes they made me feel really useless, they ridiculed me for not being as strong as them, then, left me in a corner to cry on my own. I didn't earn any sympathy by being a girl in fact it seemed quite the opposite. Our house felt lovely when the fires were lit, especially the one in our front room. It brought back such happy memories of the family when Father was still at home, although our parents struggled at that time we still had a family home that was warm on winter nights. Now, my brothers and I were finding it impossible to do just that. We burned old shoes, rags and wood with the coal to make it last longer but everything seemed to burn so fast, it wasn't long before we were without warmth again. We spent many nights shivering with cold and going to bed early just to keep warm. Simon was wrapped up in a large woollen blanket at all times, there were no clothes to fit him and no other way to keep the chill off him. There was so much hardened excrement in and around his pram it hadn't been used for some time. I tried on numerous occasions to scrape it away from the cream vinyl lining but it was so dry I scraped more of the floral pattern off than anything else. Simon's little feet turned purple; he was so cold, yet, he never murmured unless he was hungry. He was a strong little fellow despite the fact he was so undernourished and we loved him so much.

During the winter months food was hard to find. The Co-op bins were not as well stocked as they were in summer and I found it difficult to find anything to eat. I rummaged through the neighbours' dustbins searching for scraps of food but there was very little, hardly enough to feed Simon with. Some days the bins were lined up on the streets ready to be emptied by the dustmen, which made things a little easier. If I was prepared to walk far enough I sometimes found scraps of food that I took home to my siblings and even though they complained it was covered in ashes, they found it was better than nothing. On the days I found pieces of cake and a few dry slices of bread I couldn't get home fast enough, I felt really giddy and excited. I would skip merrily along the frosted streets and whistling as I ran; it wasn't often I came across such a great find. Once I'd reached our house, it was like throwing a big party; with enough food for everyone, I felt really proud at the thought of finding it and swallowed every ounce of praise my little siblings gave me.

As the winter nights set in, David and Trevor worked fewer hours at the farm. Sometimes coming home early, this gave them little opportunity to steal potatoes and duck eggs like they used to and with less pay it created problems for us all.

To steal food now we had to take more risks which resulted in my brothers often getting caught, they got into trouble many times for breaking shop windows and gaining access to properties they shouldn't have been in. So they reverted to pushing me through neighbours' windows that they couldn't get through. I was still small and thin and a little more supple than my brothers so found it much easier. The amount of food I stole varied from one day to the next depending on the circumstances but what I did steal lasted our family some time. I hated climbing through windows into other people's houses, it made my heart pound and frightened me beyond belief, but my need to eat and feed the little ones gave me the will to do it. While I was standing in the pantries amongst all the food I often thought of the excuses I would give if I got caught, but I always hoped that I never would. It was difficult to think about getting caught when I was so hungry and my family depended on me - but I knew in my heart of hearts eventually I would.

I hated the dark nights; they seemed to last forever. Cold draughts blew fiercely through our house; without gas and electricity we were bitterly cold and suffered from what I knew as hot aches. When Mother had been at home, she had lit all three gas rings on our cooker to take the chill away but without gas we couldn't even do that. There was a time when we could just scrape up enough pennies to light one of the gas rings on the cooker but those days had passed and we had no way of keeping warm. We huddled together in our large double bed, covering ourselves with a few extra blankets and old overcoats that Father had left. Still damp and smelling of urine they didn't really help to keep us warm but the odour left on Father's coats helped to comfort us. I lay in our bed looking up into the dark, tears rolling down my cheeks. I cried silently so as not to alarm my siblings. Holding a large lump in the back of my throat, I swallowed hard to stop myself from crying aloud, stretching my arms around all three little ones I hugged them soundly, as I cradled us all to sleep.

There were many times when I woke up crying during the night, wondering why I was so cold and hungry, and looking over my sleeping siblings, I thought back to the times when I had been warm and well cared for. I remembered the hospital where I had been ill for many weeks but felt cosy and warm and fed well every day and recalled our last Christmas, when I felt the warmth of the glowing fire on my cheeks and tasted the chestnuts that father roasted before we went to bed. I remembered our holiday at Dovedale and the pretty white cottage in the country where the sun shone all day long and I remembered my very first taste of Marmite and honey that trickled off my toast. Then my thoughts drifted to the day I came home to an empty house, dirty and cold, no welcome from our mother, just a short, scribbled note addressed to Miss Woodward. As she silently read the note her eyes drifted down the page in a manner of disgust and her expression changed from her usual happy glow to a look of forlorn hopelessness.

She looked down at me, a large bunch of flowers in my hand, unable to speak, her expression said it all. I knew my mother, only too well. I remember I hadn't wanted to come back to this, I knew before I was six years old that any happiness I had ever experienced was in the past and I knew only too well what the future held for me. I wanted to leave there and then with Miss Woodward but the time wasn't right. I wished with all my heart that she would take me with her, but, for all the sadness, heartache and fear I had locked up inside me, I couldn't tell her. I didn't know how. I placed the flowers I had bought for Mother on the kitchen chair knowing they would still be there in weeks to follow. Waving goodbye to Miss Woodward I felt the warmth of my tears trickling down my cheeks.

I couldn't count how many times I had traded in all my hopes and wishes of ever owning a dolls pram for a slice of bread or a piece of cake but now I was willing to trade in much more than that – my mother for someone else's. I don't recall how many times I had wished my best friend's mum had been mine instead of hers or our next-door neighbours' mother was ours instead of theirs, but still, I remained hopeful.

—◊◊—

CHAPTER 6

A Penny for the Guy

I wasn't very old, when I began to realize that no amount of hoping and wishing would ever change anything. If I wanted to survive the cold, cruel abuse and abandonment, then I had to hide away my weaknesses and radiate strength, so that I could be sure my younger siblings and I had the chance to pull through. From that moment on, I encouraged the little ones to enjoy every seasonal celebration and to take advantage of every situation. When bonfire night drew near, we used Father's old clothes to build a giant Guy Fawkes. We stuffed him until he was quite plump and used one of Father's old trilbies to put on his head. We collected money from neighbours, clubs and pubs and even from the folk that passed by us in the streets. A penny for the guy wasn't fun for us, but a desperate attempt to feed ourselves. We trailed the streets dragging the guy as we chattered excitedly about everything we wished for, from a big bag of coal to keep us warm, to a tin of tomato soup that we'd enjoy for our suppers – not, I suppose the usual chatter for children of our age. As the pubs began to turn out, I knew it was time to head home. I was tired and Simon had got so heavy I could barely carry him. After carrying him all night I often cried as I felt the desperate struggle to keep him attached to me the best way I could, just so I could get him home with us. It was so cold I wished many times for a pair of gloves like Anne wore, and thought of everything we could buy if we had collected enough money; but they were just dreams, children's dreams.

Apart from a little that we hid, David took sole charge of any money we took home, and being the eldest he decided what it was spent on. If Carol sprung a visit, she took the money for herself. She seemed to know the nights we went out with the guy and appeared holding her hands out, as if she was entitled to every penny we had collected. Sometimes she even crept up on us outside the clubhouse where we begged regularly, she knew we always begged there as it was close to Nightingales shop and gave us the opportunity to spend some of the money before we arrived home. She often took every penny we had, just because she could, she'd hardened to circum-stances like ours and didn't care much about us or our predicament. Eventually it came to the stage where I had to hide some of the money inside my shoe so we could eat - a small bag of bonfire toffee or a bag of chips to share was the excitement of the night; making all those hours of standing about in the rain, worthwhile.

I considered Carol very lucky. She always looked clean and well fed, enjoying the freedom of visiting pubs and clubs with her boyfriend, Barry, but I didn't like her much, especially when she'd been drinking. Nor did I like the foul smell of beer on her breath or the waft of cigarettes as she hung over me, ordering me around and dictating where I should or shouldn't be at that time of night. What did she know? She was warm and well cared for and a damned sight happier than I was. I watched as she laughed and giggled her way back into the warm clubs seeking approval from Barry after she'd robbed us of every penny we had.

I hadn't realized how selfish she was until that happened. I'd always thought of her as being the most generous and considerate of my siblings but in retrospect, she was only generous with the others' belongings. We could have anything that belonged to David and Trevor and even steal Anne's chocolates when Carol was around, arguing on our behalf; she acquired all sorts of things for us. But we couldn't have anything of hers. When she had sweets, crisps or anything we liked, she kept them close by her side, determined not to allow anyone to take them from her. I remember how she served herself the largest portion of food when Mother still lived at home and anything she found was as good as hers. When I think back to the most difficult times of my life, I think it was the destitution that brought out the best in me.

—∿—

CHAPTER 7

Gyp

When Mother finally returned home to collect her last suitcase of clothing, I sensed it was her final visit and knew I wouldn't be seeing her again. She tied up all the loose ends before she left and because she knew she wasn't coming back, she had Gyp our black and white collie, taken away and put to sleep. That was the worst blow of all. He had been a good and faithful pet but he had grown old and terribly weak. He walked slowly and a little off balance, his eyesight was failing and he began to have fits. He was extremely ill but I loved him more than anything. He had been my shadow and my true friend for the full nine years I had been alive, he was soft and gentle and had joined in all our fun. He had followed me to school on my very first day and thereafter totally ignoring my unintentionally aggressive demands for him to stay at home. Every morning the whole school was in uproar as he followed me through the school gates, down the drive and through the main entrance, and even when I didn't allow him through the door onto the corridors another child did. It was difficult not to; Gyp being so determined and all. He loved school and the children laughed when they saw him but my teacher was adamant that school was no place for a family dog, and because his presence disrupted so many classes I was always advised to take him home. I think everyone on our estate loved Gyp. Most of the older children had grown up around him so he was readily accepted in and amongst the community and given a fair amount of respect by everyone. In those days dogs were allowed to roam free so long as they weren't aggressive or vicious but my teachers drew a line to him attending school. I must admit he wasn't the most obedient dog, no sooner had I taken him home and was halfway up the hill on my way back to school he was behind me and I'd have to take him home again, he was a funny dog. He had shared everything with me, the good, the bad, every warm day and cold night that we suffered, he had been part of me and my family all my life so it was difficult to let him go.

Although my memories become a little clouded at times, I still recall Mother allowing him to be prodded and pushed towards the little white van whilst I cried out to stop the old man from hitting him. Had she forgotten how faithful Gyp was? How he always knew and was ready to meet her off the bus at night?

Gyp struggled, he didn't understand and I cried so much I couldn't even see the shape of him through my tears. The van doors slammed shut and he was gone. At that moment I really hated her. I called out Gyp's name as loud as I could and ordered the old man to set him free but it was no good, Gyp was caged up and I was heartbroken. The old man charged Mother £1, climbed back into his van, then, drove away. I stood by and watched Carol cry but I was so sure my tears ran much deeper. I hated them for this. Gyp was the only thing I had loved that had never hurt me and he had loved me unconditionally. I knew I would never forget him and never forgive those that let him go without allowing me to say goodbye. They had sent away the very thing that held me together; by killing him they killed a very large part of me.

Mother hadn't even waited for me to stop crying before she took hold of her suitcase. She promised she'd come back but I wasn't listening. I had never felt the way I felt about her that day. Unlike the previous times when she had walked away from us, I was happy for her to leave. I knew she didn't love me like I had loved her. My love for Gyp overpowered everything. I crawled under our kitchen table and lay down on Gyp's blanket, his smell all around me and cried even more. I cried so much that day, I lost the will to stay awake and slept on Gyp's blanket for hours, caring nothing for anyone but for my special friend who I had lost. Then David and Trevor came home from the farm and they called out his name just as they always had done and I cried some more. Each morning I got out of bed, thought about Gyp and cried uncontrollably. I don't know how many weeks or months I cried myself to sleep each night but one thing I do know, he will never leave my thoughts. The memories of that day have haunted me all my life, as I sit here and cry I shed as many tears for him as I did back then remembering what it was like to have him as my best friend.

When Mother left us that day, she left a little food behind as she always had done. It wasn't much, but then it never was, just a few Oxo cubes, bread, butter, milk and sugar and the remainder of a large piece of cheese. She had bought the food earlier that day so she could have a sandwich before she moved on. We ate too, simply because we were there at the same time and eager to join her. Mother had a habit of having regular meals such as lunch at mid-day, unlike us she wasn't used to going without. Being a sizable woman it took a fair amount to keep her feeling full, so most of what she bought she consumed well before she left that day. Most of the memories I have of Mother are of her sitting at our kitchen table eating cooked breakfasts; bacon, eggs and tomatoes while we stood around waiting for the bacon rind she always left on the side of her plate.

As I sit here writing these words I cannot recall sitting down at the table with Mother or Father when we lived together as a family. My memories are all too clear, we stood by the side of the kitchen table crying and even begging for food while they ate their meals in front of us. Although we shared their leftovers, their leavings didn't fill us. Supper was usually our main meal after the activity of the day had come to a standstill and everyone was tired of running around, then we were fed. Carol and I usually cooked suppers, varying the meals from the usual mashed potatoes and turnip to mashed potatoes and soup. When food ran out, Mother used to send me to Nightingales shop to buy the usual four bags of crisps to share between all of us. David and Carol always had a full bag each, but Trevor, Andrew, Lorraine and I shared two bags between us. I don't recall Simon being born at that time, but I clearly remember squabbling over the amount of crisps we were given and who got to keep the bag. For some reason, we younger children were under the illusion that there were more crisps left in the bag as it always seemed to take more time to eat those than it did the portion left on the table, but thinking back, the larger portion was more likely to have been the pile on the table that everyone was so willing to give up. It seemed that I was always the one forced into walking to the shop when it was late; everyone knew I was nervous and frightened of the dark but they still chose me to go. At times it was like living amongst a pack of wild dogs and I was the runt of the litter with everyone snarling and barking at me until I did everything they said. My fear of the dark and of wide open spaces caused me to hyperventilate until I dripped with sweat, anxious and frightened. I often wondered why Mother insisted I should be the one to go. Being treated like that always made me panic and my fear regularly got the better of me, I was an outcast and I knew it. Carol was like Mother's right hand, she couldn't wait to punish me, knocking me towards the front door; she would kick me through it to go to the shop just to save Mother a job. I had to obey, I was too small not to. I cried my way up the garden path and all the way to the shop, looking and listening for any sudden movements or unfamiliar sounds, fearful of what I might see or hear. Once my eyes had got accustomed to the dark I felt a whole lot better, but it still didn't rid me of those feelings of hate I had growing inside me. I never stopped looking back at her, thinking how much she must hate me. I was hurt and upset and couldn't think for the life of me why it was always me who received her punches. Was I really so different ?

—◦—

CHAPTER 8

My Father's Tears

By the time I was nine years old I had changed so much I barely knew myself. I had been left to care for my younger siblings for so long that I had hardened and had stopped crying and wishing for Mother's return. I had accepted that I was the one responsible for the three little ones. David and Trevor looked after themselves and Carol only returned to the house when she wanted something, although, she knew there was very little left to take.

In the middle of the long winters when the house was really cold, we chopped up everything we could find, including chairs and any items we considered ideal for the fire and apart from the larger pieces of furniture we thoroughly stripped the house bare.

Being left alone, I had learnt to do a lot of things I hadn't done before. David had shown me how to use Father's saw and Trevor taught me how to climb the lamp post on the corner of our street, so I could steal the bulb each time it was fitted with a new one. I taught myself how to stew the blackberries we picked from the hedgerows and was a dab hand at making lumpy custard.

I had grown much bigger and had outgrown a lot of the girls' clothing, my dresses where too short and my duffle coat fitted young Andrew. I changed my shoes to some that had once belonged to my older sisters and had found some more clothes to fit Lorraine, they where old and shabby and disgustingly smelly but they covered her. Andrew had taken to wearing anybody's - too big, too small, he wasn't fussy. I searched through Mother's wardrobe and found some of her old dresses in tatters, far too big for me, but tucked up into a belt, I wore them anyway. Having a large family, Mother had got into the habit of hoarding everything so it gave us plenty to delve into. I couldn't help feeling sorry for Andrew, whenever he found a pair of trousers that fit him Trevor made him take them off, so he could wear them to the farm. Trevor had very few garments to fit him and reverted back to the wet muddy trousers he had previously worn to the farm. During the winter months the caked on mud didn't dry, this left all the boys fighting each other for dry clothing.

Simon, had learned to walk, a little off balance, but he was getting there. We stole clothing from washing lines to fit him and I remember we once stole a small tricycle from a garden near the park. We took it to the police station alleging we had found it, just like the family had taught us and after a few weeks had passed and it hadn't been claimed, we got it back, as we knew we would. It was one of the few things we stole that we didn't really need, but the temptation proved far too great. We had never had a bike before and it was certainly easier than carrying him around, so we took advantage of it.

Lorraine had grown, so had her hair, she spoke with a lisp and had begun roaming the streets on her own. She made friends with the policeman's wife who lived down our street, often visiting her and bringing home bananas and large pieces of cake she was proud to share with us. But as time elapsed she got defensive and fought when I took a little for Simon and myself. There had been many days when that was the only food we had and only needed a little just to tide us over, but Lorraine couldn't comprehend that. Andrew had grown so much he was able to climb the highest of walls into the orchard at the bottom of our estate but was still unable to climb the apple trees that bore the most fruit. So he still came home empty handed.

I recall Father visiting our house when Mother had made her final decision not to return home to us. He didn't speak much, but then he never did. He walked towards the house with all of us hanging on to the bottom of his jacket, pulling and tugging him further into the house as we let out screeches of delight. We had always been pleased to see him, even when Mother had been at home he lifted our spirits and brought out the best in us, just by being kind.

It had been such a long time since we had seen him and I hoped he had come home to stay, but I realised that he hadn't when he began collecting his tools from the garden shed. He looked sad and lonely as he reluctantly gathered the rest of his overcoats from the hallway and put them into his car, then, he walked around the house slowly, his face full of sadness. Circling the whole of downstairs before sitting down on the only chair that was left in the kitchen - he lowered his head into the palms of hands and cried. We all fell silent. None of us ever remembered seeing Father cry before. I moved up close to him and asked what was wrong, but he couldn't speak. I placed my arms around his neck and held him tight as the others shuffled closer towards me. Father raised his head and looked down at me, his eyes red and swollen and filled with tears he held out his arms and said *"Come here little Mother"*. I couldn't move any further forward and my siblings were almost attached to me, so he lifted me onto his lap and wrapped his arms around all four of us squeezing really tight. He repeated the word sorry over and over again, but being so young I didn't really understand what he was sorry for.

Father asked about Mother so I told him what I knew. Then he got up and again walked around our house as if he were lost, sighing and shaking his head from side to side. He walked steadily into the kitchen and out through the back door that led into the garden where his trestle bench was still standing, and he sawed the large pieces of wood that had proven too tough for us to saw. He built a large stock of small logs at the foot of the door and made a fire in the kitchen with the bundle of sticks he had chopped earlier.

He fetched bread and tins of soup from the Co-op that he warmed and gave us in cups that had broken handles, then, drove us to Stavely to collect Carol from Barry's house. I had told him where she was and that she had been there on and off since Mother had left, which he didn't seem surprised about. Carol was overjoyed to see him, even crying a little as he wrapped his arms around her. They walked up the garden path towards the car where we sat waiting and for the first time in a long time I believe I saw deep sadness in her face.

During the journey back home he and Carol spoke about lots of things and Father repeatedly told us he couldn't stay. He promised to check on us whenever he could, but I was unhappy with that and cried all the way home. He left that same night like he said he would, looking the saddest I had ever seen him. He had given Carol money to buy food but the trust my parents had in her was inaccurately placed, and after having a little cry she left our house soon after he did, once again taking all the money with her.

It had shocked Father when he saw the state of our house and what we had become. We had never had much, even when he lived with us but we had had a far higher standard than we did at the time of his visit. He saw how the house had fallen apart and didn't have a clue how to get it all back up and running, so he left it to someone who he thought he could trust. But Carol was only a child too. At the age of fifteen she was probably less capable than I was at the age of nine. Mother always said Carol had never been the same since she fell from an upstairs window when she was little - even so she still expected her to run the home. Everyone was taking care of themselves and I knew if I wanted to survive, then, that was what I must do.

Before I had seen Father that last time, I had always thought he would come home and Mother would follow and everything would be as it should. But now I wasn't so sure. Even he had walked away, so I had nothing more left to cling to - he had been my only hope but he let me down just like everyone else; I now thoroughly mistrusted everyone. Left alone, responsible for my younger siblings I worried for their well - being. It got slightly easier once Simon had started walking but he was a baby and I found it so difficult to cope with him at times. Lorraine was almost four but still very much a baby. She had always been everyone's favourite and her long blonde hair and chubby cheeks won her first place in everything. There was no doubt she had been spoiled and was very demanding of me. She looked on me as her protector, nurse, carer and provider. Andrew was a little more independent. Although he was robust, he was affectionate and still needed lots of reassurance.

It was because I loved them that I knew I couldn't leave them to struggle on their own. I suppose looking back I could have been like my parents and older siblings, fed myself, looked after myself and just thought of myself, but where would the fairness have been in that? So I gave it my all, day-to-day learning and then teaching new tactics to aid our survival.

I'd thought about leaving but, there was nowhere for me to go. No one wanted me! I was just a plain little girl with nothing going for me, more of a hindrance than my brothers, so my mother had always told me. I worried more as the days passed, after seeing Father I wasn't sure what was going to happen and constantly wondered if we would ever see him again.

—◊◊—

CHAPTER 9

Being Abandoned

Despite the hardship we suffered and the time we spent foraging for food, it was amazing how we still found the energy to play. I recall playing a game called 'Splitz'. Andrew and I would face each other, just a short distance apart, our legs spread and a penknife in my hand. I threw it within the area we stood hoping it would stick in the ground close to his foot. Sometimes it travelled far enough to cause him to stretch his foot to where it had stuck upright. In turns we threw the knife until our legs where so far apart we did the 'splitz'. If we stumbled, the game began again and again. We played that game most days, but failed to see the danger in it. It was just pure luck the knife never went astray.

Our lives were full of danger - we ran across the corrugated roofs of garages, and climbed into the attic that was built into the roof of our house. We wandered up to the quarry which was a good hour's walk away from our estate, not the ideal place for children to play, but the large rocks and deep potholes made it so inviting. Used for tipping it was full of refuse and sharp pieces of scrap metal, but we played there as happy as Larry. When we were ordered to leave, we left, but returned when the coast was clear.

We spent a lot of time playing in places where we shouldn't have, doing what we shouldn't have been doing. Some days we were gone for so long, we left it too late to forage for food and went to bed hungry. It got to the stage where we knew we had to eat but as the hunger pains began to disappear our stomachs stopped reminding us. It was only when nightfall came we realised we had allowed yet another day to pass without feeding ourselves. Simon began sleeping through the night and cried far less during the day so I tended to think he was doing fine.

I remember that with time Lorraine began to speak more, she had been almost mute when Mother had lived with us. Apart from the odd swear word, which she blurted out now and again, she spoke very little, but then she had no cause to speak. When we had lived as a family everyone gave her what they thought she wanted without Lorraine so much as uttering a word. All she had to do was point and snivel and a biscuit or a sandwich would appear in her hand like magic. It may not have been what she really wanted, but it kept her quiet. Then we were abandoned and her life drastically changed, she had to learn to ask, if she didn't ask, she didn't get! It was as simple as that.

Andrew and Lorraine proved to be a real worry for me. They had a habit of disappearing from the house without telling me and went missing for hours. When I realised they were missing I chased around the house in a panic, searching high and low. Sometimes, to my relief I found them digging in our back garden scooping up all the wet mud with Mother's tablespoons and pans, the ones we cooked with, but at other times, they were nowhere to be found. I would chase around the streets with Simon in my arms searching everywhere, calling their names at the top of my voice, hoping they might hear me. I stopped by their usual haunts, spent hours searching for them, eventually finding them at someone's house scrounging food.

We fought like wild dogs when they refused to come home. We scratched, pinched and bit each other until we were so sore we would then back away from each other and trail home licking our wounds like wounded animals. We would all curse each other and they would swear at me, telling me that I wasn't the boss. I suspected they felt the way I did, all grownup and responsible! I told them it was important we all stayed together, especially when it was dark.

I remember worrying about losing them, partly because I was terrified of being left alone and because I didn't want the same thing happening to them that had happened to me, for I was aware by this time that some people weren't very nice and could harm anyone of us. Although I occasionally begged the odd coin or two from a passer-by, I no longer trusted anyone. It was amazing how I had managed to learn to read people's body language, somehow I understood who to approach and who to avoid.

By this time David and Trevor worked every day. None of us went to school, although I remember the lady from the school board calling. I was quick witted and told her Mother was out and I didn't know when she would be coming back, so she left.

We didn't have many visitors at that time, occasionally the police called but we had already been taught to lie about our parents' whereabouts and deny all knowledge of our brothers. So, whatever excuses were used we had to remember to stick to them or we would be caught out. Once when John's probation officer called, he caught me, Andrew and Lorraine plucking a pigeon in the kitchen. When I told him Mother didn't live here anymore he looked puzzled, but then a more terrifying look spread over his face as he noticed the amount of feathers that were scattered around the kitchen and we had stuck to our fingers. I told him we were cooking the bird for our suppers but he was obviously revolted by it. He explained that we couldn't eat the bird as it was riddled with maggots. I didn't believe him and the doubt must have shown on my face as he attempted to demonstrate with a poker that the neck was full of maggots, crawling up from the pigeon's stomach. We had noticed some movement from the bird's chest when we first began to pluck but continued nevertheless, occasionally jumping back terrified at the thought of it still being alive but quickly we continued plucking, satisfied that it was dead. Before he left he insisted on taking the pigeon away and once outside he threw it to the bottom of our garden. Satisfied that he had done the right thing he then left our house without fulfilling any obligation to us. I was devastated. We had carried that dead pigeon all the way from Ward's farm believing we had something to eat.

Everything took a turn for the worse. We weren't managing to feed ourselves and I hadn't seen David or Trevor for some time. Life was becoming even more desperate and I began to worry. We were, by this time, a little barbaric - it came with a heartfelt desperation and as time moved on, we and life, got much worse.

I picked up on something the probation officer said about John being released from prison but at that moment in time I wasn't interested. I didn't even know what prison was, so I didn't understand what he was talking about, only that he seemed desperate to see Mother before John's release. Everything he said went in one ear and out the other, except the word 'John'- that name registered in my mind like a bolt of lightning. I panicked and immediately started to fret. I became so distressed I cried at the thought of seeing him again. I had been able to forget him for a while but now his ginger hair and freckles and all the pain he had caused me came flooding back. I found it difficult to sleep at night and lay awake worrying and crying, wondering who would protect me now. With too many memories of him lurking around my bedroom, abusing me and hurting me I was too scared to stay there. I got so frightened I carried Simon and woke Andrew and Lorraine so they could follow me outside, where I'd laid a blanket in an unused flowerbed enabling us to sleep in our front garden. We covered ourselves with blankets that Andrew dragged alongside him and stayed hidden from everyone that passed us by. I felt safe in my father's garden, it reminded me of the happy times I'd had as a younger and more innocent child.

After not seeing Anne for some time, she began visiting again during the weekends, but she didn't stay for long, the house was so dirty she wrinkled her nose at the foul smell we had created and left as soon as she could.

She looked sad, her eyes filled with tears as she glanced around, taking note of all the destruction we had caused. We had wrecked her piano that once stood proudly in our front room. Her heart sank and I could see that she couldn't find the words to speak. She played a few notes checking the extent of the damage then burst into tears. She didn't swear or curse like Carol would have done but sat at the piano as if her heart had sunk to her feet, she couldn't even look at us.

I remember watching as she stood up and straightened her skirt, being careful not to mark her beautifully tailored clothing with grease and dirt that was splashed on what remained of our furniture as she walked around the house looking for something to wrap around her. Rummaging through Mother's sideboard she pulled out a slightly soiled piece of cloth and tied it around her waist, while she boiled a kettle and filled the kitchen sink with warm water to bathe Simon. He must have been close to a year old then as he was able to sit in the sink without her supporting him.

Once she had washed his hair and thoroughly cleaned him up, she dressed him in new clothing she had bought especially for him; socks, shoes and a brand new coat as well. He didn't look much like my brother once she'd finished with him, but just like the baby Mother had brought home from the hospital; he looked lovely. When he was all spruced up and ready to go, Anne cradled him in her arms and proudly carried him out of the house. I stood in the jamb of the door watching them leave - wishing I was going with them. But Anne never failed to remind me, as she turned to close our garden gate that I shouldn't follow her and I must remain at home. Under no circumstances was I to go down to Margaret's, where she and Simon had been invited and I hadn't to make a fuss.

Ron pulled up in his beautiful sky blue car, got out of the driver's side and walked to the passenger's side to open the door for Anne. I sensed the way she moved she didn't want Ron to see the little waifs and strays she was leaving behind. She moved quickly climbing into the car and pulled Simon back onto her knee, as she positioned herself on the seat, quickly kissing Ron as he climbed back into the driver's seat, and he then drove away. She didn't wave – she was too ashamed. He hadn't met us and I knew while we lived there he never would. Anne was proud, but certainly not of us, only of herself and her own achievements and of course Simon. She hated the thought of being part of our family and built her life as far away from us as she could. She hated her surname and anything that associated her with it and made it clear to me that when she married Ron, she would no longer be one of us.

Anne was lucky to have had a good upbringing. She was sixteen years my senior and had received a good education and private music lessons. She played the piano beautifully and was everything I wanted to be, I loved her and looked up to her and hoped that one day I would be just like her. She spent many years contributing towards the upkeep of our house, helping in ways she thought were most important, but buying Christmas presents and the occasional pair of shoes didn't help pay the rent or keep us from starving. Anne's dedication was to the church, she made it quite clear the church came first and foremost in her life and nothing ever took precedence over it. She was stunning and had been lucky enough to have had such a wonderful upbringing, way before I was born. She had attended school regularly and was well educated. She played the piano so well everyone liked to hear her play, and she was everything I ever wanted to be.

Mother had struggled to provide us with all the necessities we required but when the older siblings chose their own path in life, it left her completely destitute. Up until then she had managed to keep the home in full swing, pay the rent and keep a roof over our heads. But when she was left alone, she struggled to pay the bills and it soon became apparent she was fighting a losing battle. I still remember the arguments between Mother and some of my older siblings, regarding money and their wishes to keep their own wages, for although they still lived with us, they were reluctant to part with enough money to make a difference. They were very lucky, each one of them had somewhere else to go and someone else to run to but when our home finally broke up, we six little ones weren't so fortunate.

Although most of my family knew we had been abandoned, Anne was the only one that maintained contact with us, although irregular. She visited some weekends but didn't stay overnight like she had done in the past. Her love for Simon brought her back to the house when she did visit but just a quick visit from an older sister wasn't enough for him, he needed more than that. He needed a mother, a regular mother, one that could love him, clothe him, and take care of him. A mother he could rely on. He needed a home, somewhere safe with someone who cared enough not to leave or abandon him. He needed a lot more than just me. It was difficult trying to deliver all those things when I was so young. At the age of nine I hadn't ever thought about the feelings I had for my younger siblings, they were my family and it was something inside me that helped me pull them through, I loved and cared for them and it was this that kept them safe.

I had learned to believe in a lot of things during the first decade of my life but the prayers I had learned in church were the most important to me, it was these that kept my spirits alive both day and night when I spent all that time alone in my bedroom. I sang 'Jesus wants me for a sunbeam' so many times I heard the echo of my own voice in my sleep. I learned that everyone has a path to follow and believed I was following mine. During my journey I hoped that I wouldn't come to harm, and although there was always a risk that I may, I still continued that journey, taking with me those closest to my heart Andrew, Lorraine and Simon. They became my life and soul, needing me as I needed them. Together we traveled this incredible journey hoping one day we'd be saved.

I had fond memories of Anne during previous years, dressing Andrew, Lorraine and myself for church on Sunday mornings. She had once loved to take us with her, teaching us things from the bible and songs that she sang, but she changed and hid us away from the people and friends that she knew. We weren't allowed to be her family anymore although she tried to show some feeling for us; her dignity was far more important to her. Although I was young, I understood the difference between Anne and myself. I was dirty and uncared for, she was clean and fresh. I spoke with vulgarity, she spoke with self-assurance, I was ignorant and rude, she, was knowledgeable and well mannered. Why would she want anyone to know that a small part of her was also a part of, me? Anne gave me hope each time she returned home. There was never a better sight than seeing her standing in the opening of our front door, she beamed like a huge ray of light. I prayed so hard for her return each Friday – I almost sensed the times when she wouldn't and thanked God when she did. When she returned to us she fed us egg mayonnaise and banana sandwiches knowing it was our favourite and sometimes treated us to potted beef. It was a feast! It was strange how filling our stomachs gave us the will to forget. All that had happened previously suddenly became distant and unreal. We laughed and played like children do, but it wasn't for long - two days was all we had. We had no idea what the future held for us. We lived for the moment and for that moment we were happy.

I suppose Anne came home as often as she could but even she knew it wasn't enough to keep us from starving. We had become so thin and bony even our neighbours began to show concern. I remember the Creswell family who lived in the house adjacent to ours, passing comment to other neighbours about our unhealthy appearances.

Mrs Creswell had been so kind in the past, sparing me a shilling for both our gas and electric meters, I dared not approach her for anything else. Her son, Terry, often cast out the change from his pockets as he passed our house, watching and sneering as we scrambled around the pavement searching for the coins that helped keep us alive, his face showing a little pity but more of revulsion, like so many that passed by. It was at this time of my life, I first noticed fear and repulsion in people's faces. Supposedly charitable people of status and good character, who found it hard to look a child like me in the eyes as they quickened their pace to pass by me. It was only then that I fully understood the meaning of "being abandoned". We were alone and I knew for sure the friends and neighbours that we once had, now feared everything we stood for.

I couldn't imagine what they saw when they stood looking at us, but whatever it was it created fear and panic in their eyes. My small family of waifs and strays were living with hunger and destitution, we were the tiny outcasts of a generation neglected and abandoned. Our friends' denial became our worst enemy, but their own safety net. Their rational thoughts had become so distorted it affected their understanding of poverty and neglect and the whole picture of so many children in need created fear within their hearts and their minds.

It was that same fear that caused neighbours to close their doors on me when I called for help thereafter. The few people I had once relied upon now saw me as nothing, but a menace. My siblings and I had become so weak and desperately low it took us all our time to walk across the road to the shops. Frank had managed to change the whole set up of the Co-op which made it almost impossible to steal food from there, but fortunately our reliance on his goodwill was still worthy. He still sorted out the over-ripened fruit, leaving it in brown paper bags on top of the fruit boxes, awaiting our collection. We were so hungry we ate the fruit as we got it and gave no thought of tomorrow. Gorging it in to our mouths, we ate as much as we could while we could. Each one of us tried to swallow more than the other, hoping it would ease away the painful griping pangs that had been building up during the days we went without.

—◊—

CHAPTER 10

The Fairground

I recall one morning we were making our usual trip to the Co-op and there, in full view, stuck to the glass window was a large, colourful poster advertising 'All THE FUN OF THE FAIR'. An automatic thrill of excitement whirled in and around my stomach as I took in every detail of the poster. It had been such a long time since we had had anything to look forward to so it took a while for the details to sink in. Then I screamed with delight as a sudden burst of hysteria ran through my bones, and grabbing Andrew and Lorraine by their hands, I whirled them around and around, spinning with all the vigour I could muster. All I could think of was my older sister Julie and her friend Celia. I couldn't wait to see them. I had forgotten Mother and Father had agreed to let Julie travel with the fair as soon as she left school. Worrying about the family I'd forgotten all about her, but suddenly I felt so excited, that very day I made a trip to the fairground hoping to find her, but I found nothing. There were posters splashed over boards and gates advertising all the rides, so I knew it was on its way.

The excitement of it all made me feel quite sick and I forgot all about my hunger pangs and desperation.

I stayed at the ground all day and most of the night playing alongside my siblings, waiting and wondering when it was going to arrive. Each day that passed my heart sank and I walked home heartbroken, dragging my siblings behind me. I wondered whether the fair was ever going to come.

It wasn't just the fair that filled my head with excitement but the thought of seeing Julie. It had been such a long time since we had seen her I had almost forgotten what she looked like and had she not been so dissimilar to my other siblings I would have had no recollection of her at all, but I always remembered her being good to me so I held her close to my heart.

Mother and Father had agreed to Julie joining the fair more or less as soon as she left school at the age of fourteen, and it was the poster that swept memories of my sister back to me, reminding me that Celia had taken her to live and work with them as part of their family, so there was still a little hope for us. I knew Julie would be pleased to see us and I thought if I told her we were on our own she would come home with us. But I wasn't sure if the fair was ever going to arrive. Many days had passed since I first saw the poster. I began to wonder if we had somehow missed it. I hadn't taken stock of dates and I had no idea what month we were in so I didn't bother to walk to the fairground again.

Then a few days later I was surprised at the amount of parents and children walking past our house laughing and giggling, eating candy floss and toffee apples - then I knew it was here. The excitement I felt when I saw them racing towards the ground gave me all the strength I needed to gather up my siblings and venture down to the fairground one more time, in the hope of finding Julie. I approached the gates with my eyes wide open singing all the songs that were being played over the loudspeakers. I recall The Carnival is Over being played as we approached the speedway. My eyes filled with tears as the brightly coloured lights and the sweet smell of candy gave me a rare feeling of warmth and contentment. I stopped and gazed for a while at the thrill of the action, wondering at all the activity. I became so enthralled with the excitement of it all I momentarily forgot about Julie and wandered aimlessly around the large boxed stalls and brightly coloured hoop-las, as my eyes scanned the ground for any half-eaten hot dogs or toffee apples that might feed our cravings and satisfy our hunger.

We gathered around the Waltzer and the speedway watching as each ride thundered around the tracks, and sensing a little fear, I trembled. I don't know why I got excited at the thought of actually having a ride as I knew only too well it would never happen. I had visited the fair every year and whilst the music, the noise and the vibrating ground beneath our feet gave me an excited giddiness within my stomach, I still didn't know what it was like to take a ride.

I so loved the fair, the twinkling of the lights and the aromas that came from the large selection of foods made me think of Christmas, warm, colourful and full of joy. The ever-changing music and the delightful laughter of the children helped me to forget my worries and I felt happy.

A glimpse of Andrew, Lorraine and Simon's little faces made me realise that for the first time in a long time they were all smiling. As the crowds began to thin down, the workers behind the stalls pulled down their canvases and tied them with rope, as pulling and tugging they secured their lot. With an occasional whistle and quick movement of their hands they indicated with a visible display to turn out the lights.

The rides were still and quiet, there were no more thundering wheels, the music and the sweet smell of candy had long disappeared and I wondered had it all been a dream?

We hadn't seen Julie all night and I glanced around the fairground expecting everything to disappear, but as we shuffled through the dark dusty grounds making our way to the gate, I dared to spin around one more time and was overjoyed to see that everything was still there.

The sudden sound of a man's voice bought me back to reality. He was aggressive and ordered us get out, *Come back tomorrow when it's open",* he said. His voice was sharp and registered authority, and then I knew everything was for real. I thought about asking him if he knew Celia, but before I could speak he again ordered us to move on, *"Go on get out of here come back tomorrow when we open".* Smiling, I grabbed a firmer grip of my siblings' hands and cursed him for being a fool. I dragged my siblings through the gate and up the road and whispered half-heartedly, *"Don't worry, we'll see her tomorrow".* The walk back to our house was one of the worst I had ever experienced. Over a period of time we had grown a little weak through the lack of food, but tonight we had gorged ourselves with so many scraps of food we had picked up off the ground, we were weak with plenty and pushed ourselves to finish the walk home. When we finally arrived back we were so tired we went straight up to bed and drifted off to sleep with the unusual feeling of comfort and peace. For the first time in a long time I slept the whole night without pain and free of worry. There was no whimpering or stirring from Simon and for once no bad dreams for me.

I don't remember making our usual trip across to the Co-op the following morning, but I do recall jumping out of bed first thing and rushing out of the house to make another journey down to the fairground. Food wasn't much of a problem when the fair was in town. We often found half eaten bread cobs and a hot dog or two thrown about the grounds and sometimes even a toffee apple or a clump of candy floss that had been dropped by careless children. Yes, food was quite plentiful when the fair was in town.

The next day we arrived on the grounds hours before the rides would begin but I dare say half the children in Eckington had too. There were lots of girls standing around the rides, talking, laughing and dancing to the music that had already begun. I dashed over to the cake-walk as the machine was switched on, it was my favourite and I watched the girls line up to pay and my eyes scanned each and every one of them. They were people I knew, but none gave me the time of day. All at once my eyes became fixed as I recognized our sister Carol. I smiled to myself as I realised she wouldn't have missed this for the world. She stood at the far end of the cakewalk shuffling and dancing as she moved on with each step, laughing and joking with the boys who manned the waltzer. She hadn't seen us standing at the foot of the ride, and I was wary and became more than a little frightened. I'd always been frightened of her and I knew she would hate the thought of me being there. I readied myself and stood my ground waiting for her to pounce. I knew she'd try and force me to leave but as she no longer lived with us I didn't feel she had any right to insist. There was never any doubt in my mind that when she chose to leave our house she did so solely for her own good, therefore relinquishing all responsibility for us. Every time I had seen her since she had left home she had looked happy, clean and well cared for. At that moment in time all I wanted from her was some information on Julie; nothing else seemed to matter.

As she moved around the cakewalk to the right hand side, she glared as our eyes met and looked at me in disgust but then seemed to ponder for a while as she took in the overall sight of Andrew, Lorraine and Simon, who were huddled around me. Gradually her face glowed with a blushing tinge of red as she signed with her finger for us to move around to the side where no one could see us. Obeying her command, I put my hands around my siblings and shunted them in between the waltzer and the cakewalk praying that when she followed, she wouldn't be too violent towards me.

I was at the limit of my endurance and was certain I couldn't take another beating but Carol never changed and she came storming through the crowds, grabbing me by the neck and in her usual tone and manner of speaking asked, *"What the fuck are you doing here?"* I yanked my head away from her only too ready to fight back, and yelled, *"I'm looking for our fucking Julie"*. It wasn't often that I answered back when she was standing so close but I had become so desperate that I no longer felt scared of her.

At the sound of my high pitched yelling and cursing a square door flung wide open and a figure began to unfold from a small boxed type dwelling. As she stood upright and turned towards the light I saw it was my sister Julie. She gave us all a kind smile and spoke softly to us but her words didn't register. I didn't get time to say what I wanted to say as Carol was so angry that I'd bad mouthed her, she just wanted to kill me. Julie smiled and asked in a pleasant tone of voice why Andrew was wearing a dress, I looked up at her and shrugged my shoulders. She laughed and rubbed the top of my head with her hand, just like Father used to then advised me to take the younger ones home. Not being able to understand why she didn't want me to stay, I hung my head in a contrary manner with no intention of doing as I was told.

Carol had gone back to the cakewalk and I didn't want to go back home, but Julie called her over and instructed her to see us home. Carol's face flared with anger as she bent over and grabbed Simon. She took him into her arms and flung him to one side, resting him on her hip, then brutally kicked me as far in front of her as she could. She walked in haste dragging Lorraine by the hand, leaving Andrew on his own to walk behind her. She knew he couldn't keep up with her but it was something she did purposely to warrant the occasional smack in the mouth she gave him. Once we had reached the Recreation ground she was so angry she almost knocked me down as she threw Simon into my arms. I despised her for bullying me, she was so full of hate she inflicted pain without ever thinking about the damage she caused me.

I carried Simon in my arms while the others followed, occasionally stopping to rest wondering if I dared return to the fair. But she knew me too well. I turned to look over my shoulder to see her watching me. I had forgotten that my tricks were once her tricks and practically everything I knew I'd learnt from her. Before I reached the park I dared to turn once more but there she was, stood as if she were frozen, watching me like a cat watching a mouse so, I gave her the game and walked on, quickening my step, I had accepted defeat.

When we arrived home I was surprised to find David and Trevor back from the farm so early. It was unusual but I was happy to see them, I felt much safer when they were around. We hadn't seen them for some time so I noticed many changes in their appearances. David, who was usually quite plump, had thinned down and his hair had grown over his eyes. Trevor had grown taller and his hair was far bushier than I had ever seen it before, it had changed from auburn to a dirty nut brown, David's was still black but he himself looked pale and worn.

I told them the fair was in town but they had already heard. They were overjoyed and asked excitedly about all the rides, and constantly quizzed me about the speedway and the dodgems and asked occasionally if Julie was there. They kicked off their Wellington boots and quickly got changed into some of John's old clothes that were obviously too big for them, but dry, and rummaged some old shoes from the kitchen cupboard. Then off they went, through the front door and down the street, running as fast as their legs would carry them.

I felt excited just watching them. I had never seen David raise so much as a smile since Mother left. For the first time since that day, I watched him play around and laugh out loud. Since our abandonment there had been a horrible and solemn atmosphere in and around our house but tonight it felt different, we were all happy, bright eyed and because Julie was near we assumed everything was going to turn out just fine.

David had always been the most reserved member of our family, he was quiet and hardly ever mixed with me like my younger brothers did. He had never associated himself with many of us, yet he seemed to look up to Julie. I think he loved her, just as we all did and yet he never showed any kind of warmth towards her. Apart from bringing home an occasional bar of chocolate for Simon, when the farmer paid his wages, I don't recall him ever getting close to anyone. Yet, apart from John we all had this unusual and sincere respect for David. I always remember him being reasonable and fair and he didn't willingly join in any games that may include criticism or ridicule towards anyone else. Yet I recall John kicking and punching him, to the extent that he drew blood. I recall David calling out for Mother as John repeatedly punched and kicked him in the face just because he wouldn't punch him back. I felt sick with hatred each time I set eyes on John and had wished so many times that he would lose the fights he had deliberately caused. But he was strong and so bitterly twisted, he always won hands down every time and David stood no chance of defending himself against that bully. I had often stood and watched him receive blow after blow, I would watch as John clenched his fist and ripped into him as if he were a punch bag. I'd seen blood running from David's eyebrows and nose so many times as he cried silent tears simply because he felt too ashamed to cry aloud.

John had been totally out of control for a long while now, he believed he was our dictator and he certainly had the power that went with being a dictator. He had controlled all of us and our parents from as far back as I could remember; he'd been totally unfair and infinitely

cruel and proud of the fact that no one had any authority over him. Today I hang my head in disgust as I recall
the times my parents pleaded with him to behave, but he
was unwilling to do as they asked and could never resist
that one final blow, the blow that made David cry
uncontrollably. We had all felt the agonizing pain of
John's repeated blows and knew that David only put up
with them to protect us weaker ones. Both our parents
knew that John had a psychopathic personality and this
was the reason they feared him, they'd given him everything but took nothing from him hoping that spoiling
him would help to change his personality, but they were
wrong. John's very existence impacted on so many innocent people's lives, he left them feeling hopeless and helpless. He thrived upon destruction and terror.

By the time I was nine years old he had completely
destroyed my world and that of my siblings. He had
poisoned my mind with so much hatred and repulsion
through his vulgar fantasies and behaviours, I had
unnatural thoughts and feelings I would not have known
had it not been for his deranged personality. The few
years John had been away from home, I had been able to
walk around the house without feeling threatened and
had come to believe that he was no longer part of the
family, although at times I felt there was still part of his
aura around and contaminating the house and me.
I don't think any of my siblings thought about him
much. David didn't seem to miss him and Carol had
taken over the role of our dictator so had been happy for
him to leave. Yet everyone missed Julie. David often
mentioned her name and spoke fondly of her, and assum-
ing that he would see her down at the fairground I
wondered if he would tell her that Mother had left and

we were living on our own. She was more likely to talk to David than to me and perhaps listen to what he had to say, he was aged fourteen and more able to express himself than I was, so if anyone could get through to her, it would be him.

I couldn't resist following David and Trevor down to the fair. I knew it was only in town for a few days so I didn't want to miss any of the fun or a chance to eat - even if it meant raiding the litter bins, dotted around the grounds. I knew David had some money as I'd seen him counting it on the kitchen floor before he left, so I thought and hoped there might have been a chance of a ride or something.

By the time I'd wrapped the usual shabby blanket around Simon and tucked him into my arms, then left our house with Andrew and Lorraine following behind me, it was almost dark and getting cold. I'd searched the house for a cardigan but, by that time, we only had the clothes we stood up in. We had run out of most things and hadn't the ability to wash or dry soiled clothing. So, I made do with the only thing I had left; the simple cotton dress I used for sleeping in. Simon was lucky to still have the blanket we covered him with. Everything else of his had been saturated with urine and soiled with his excrement and left around the house to mould. The tiny vest he wore was already too small and hadn't been changed since Anne's last visit, so was heavily stained and so foul-smelling, it act as a deterrent for anyone that went near him. It was the only garment that hadn't yet grown black and green fungus!

The walk to the fair was long and the night had become bitterly cold but finally we reached the last street and I could see the twinkling of the lights and hear the loud music playing. We got so excited we almost ran down the last stretch of road. Simon was fast asleep in my arms so I couldn't keep up with Andrew and Lorraine but they waited for me before going through the gates. We shuffled in between the stalls and hoop-las as folks pushed past, knocking us around, until finally we headed towards the speedway where David and Trevor were talking and laughing with a group of boys they knew. As we approached the ride, David noticed us, stopped talking and looked down at me. He didn't react like Carol had, instead he put his hand into his pocket, pulled out some change, sorted it in both hands and handed me four pennies. He pointed over to a bubbly and charm machine that stood beside one of the hoop-las, and shouting to be heard above the music he told me to get some bubbly from the machine I grabbed hold of the pennies and excitedly jumped down from the steps of the speedway and ran across to the bubbly machine to collect four pence worth of bubbly – a small handful of tiny coloured balls for each penny. I gave a handful each to Andrew and Lorraine and bit Simon's portion into small pieces so he wouldn't choke on them, the last penny's worth belonged to me! All my siblings had huddled around David, tired and cold but far too excited to let it trouble them. David always showed concern for the younger ones when he was around so occasionally I was relieved of my duties and spent time resting whilst he nursed Simon.

Having popped one bubbly in our mouths and hold-ing the rest in our small fists, I walked my younger siblings around the stalls and hoop-las, leaving David and Trevor with their friends. I searched the grounds hoping to see Julie again as Celia kept crossing our paths, but it seemed Julie was a little more elusive. By the end of the night I had seen Carol but luckily her attentions were firmly fixed on the boys who operated the rides. Julie couldn't be found. I wasn't sure if David and Trevor had thought to look for her or forgotten in all the excitement.

As the evening came to an end the rides began to slow down and little by little every bright light was switched off. It was dark and already everywhere had quietened down. I heard David calling me, he told me to start walking home it was late and the fair was closing down. I gathered my small flock together and began to make my own way home. I was tired and couldn't help closing my eyes as I struggled to walk up the hill holding Simon loosely in my arms, he was fast asleep and resting his head in the crevice of my neck. Andrew and Lorraine were walking sluggishly behind me trying to cadge a lift so they didn't have to walk, but they never had much success! We hadn't even reached the path that led to the park before David and Trevor came, pounding up behind us. They were laughing and making eerie noises, joking around and generally having fun with each other. I know now I had forgotten what it was to be a child and spend time laughing and joking with them. David looked down at me as I laughed half-heartedly whilst still struggling with the weight of Simon in my arms. It was a huge relief when he took Simon from me, and careful not to stir him, he laid him back in his own arms and we carried on with our journey home. Andrew, Lorraine and I quickly trotted at David's side, trying hard to keep pace with his short, but quickened, steps. Trevor had been so used to walking at David's side to and from the farm each day that he had now mastered the art of long, stretched strides to keep in line with David's short quick ones.

David of course, was anxious to get home to catch up on his sleep before tomorrow's early morning and his next full day's work at Ward's Farm. The morning was only a few hours away and he couldn't afford to lose the job, although in reality he should have been at school, but he had to work to survive. He earned two shillings and sixpence if he worked a full week, morning until night, but there were times when the farm didn't need extra hands so both David and Trevor where laid off. This created severe desperation for us all.

When we finally reached home, none of us wasted any time getting into bed, but as I lay huddled up next to Andrew, Lorraine and Simon I couldn't help shedding a silent tear for myself. I knew the fair wasn't there for long, a day or so at the most, but I wasn't sure if that was long enough to find Julie and let her know that things had gone so horribly wrong at home.

As everyone older was so engrossed in looking after themselves, no one seemed to realise how desperate things really were for me and my younger siblings. We were far too young to work, we had nowhere to go and no other person to turn to; at times I thought we were going to die, but our lives had become so bad and desperate the thought of death no longer frightened me.

Trevor didn't receive full pay at the farm like David did but the little he did get meant that he could survive; which was more than what we could do.

I cried that night – a tear for myself and a river for my family. I knew in my own mind that at some stage, somehow all of this had to come to an end. I had grown and matured in my last year and had been forced into making a lot of decisions that a child of nine should not have been making. Sometimes I knew that when I made a decision, it was often wrong but to survive I had to follow them through.

Since Mother had left us, I had hoped for any one of my family to return to our home and help me care for my younger siblings. I had reached a stage in my young life where each morning I awoke I dreaded being alive for one more day. The continuing struggle to survive became so difficult I became too weak to fight the inevitable. My thoughts were only of my past; the abuse, neglect and abandonment were at the forefront of my mind. I knew somewhere in my small heart that if things continued as they had done over recent months none of us were going to make it. I cried out of self pity but had long since learned that crying at night didn't change what was destined to be.

I awoke the following morning to find Andrew and Lorraine already out of bed and downstairs. David and Trevor had gone to the farm as usual and Simon was sitting on the bed playing and chewing the bits of paper one of my siblings had given him. He wasn't crying but waited patiently for me to tend to him. I had to get out of bed, sort myself out and get myself moving, but it was one of those mornings my heart wasn't in it. I needed to go to the fair again but I wasn't sure if it was open as I knew it was Sunday, but it made little difference to me. I wanted to see Julie to tell her about all the things that had been happening and the struggle we were having. She couldn't have been told as I was so sure if she had known she would most definitely have come home to me.

As a horrible thought flashed through my mind, I jumped out of bed fully dressed, grabbed hold of Simon and rushed downstairs, through to the kitchen where the others were. I yelled at them with a sense of urgency in my voice, ordering them to get ready quickly. I opened the front door wide and ran through it calling out to Andrew and Lorraine to follow me. I ran as fast as I could in the direction of the fairground, puffing and panting, struggling as Simon clung tightly to my side. The distance from our house to the fairground was a long way and I ran for some time before I rested to help settle the stitch in my stomach.

I had no concept of time, whether it was morning or afternoon, I couldn't read and hadn't learnt to tell the time. I hadn't seen many people on the streets so was unable to ask anyone like I usually did, but I had to consider the little ones, so when we reached the park we rested a while. I gave Simon a little swing on my knee whilst Andrew and Lorraine played on the see-saw but once I'd got my breath back and the little ones had stopped whimpering, I continued the journey, dragging my siblings behind me. As we approached the last stretch of road, close to the fairground, I looked to see if I could see any of the rides. I panicked as I quickened my step to take a closer look but I had already begun to cry and couldn't see through the fullness of my tears, I couldn't believe that every ride had disappeared overnight. I continued running down the road towards the gates, just hoping and praying that Julie had stayed behind – I couldn't believe she would leave without saying goodbye.

As I entered the gates, I stood quiet and still, gazing through floods of tears at the emptiness of the large open grounds. Knowing we had just lost the one final chance of ever being saved I fell to my knees and lowered my head to the ground - in desperation I broke down and cried, I was devastated. With Simon clinging to my dress I cried hysterically. I knew at this point we were definitely on our own. I was sure we were finished. I felt my whole world collapse around me, no more cherished hopes or dreams of being happy and no more false beliefs of being a family again.

When I awoke that morning I'd had a strange inner feeling, a sense of disappointment and knew before I left the house that all was not well. I was a child with a dream and I couldn't let go of that one final hope of being happy, but when I found that Julie had gone I was left with nothing; no hope and no dreams. I knelt on the floor for some time, crying so many tears that a large wet patch had formed on the front of my dress. Andrew and Lorraine remained silent as they looked at me with tears in their eyes, I felt for them as they stood and watched the only security they had keel over and cry. I had been trying so hard to stay strong but found it almost impossible to carry on. I had no doubt that it was the end of the road for us.

Eventually I picked myself up off the ground and straightened my dress. Holding Simon's hand, I allowed him to walk at the side of me, as I no longer had the strength or incentive to carry him. I walked along the grounds and through the gates, heading towards the park with my emotions in tangles. I felt a sadness that I'd never felt before and yet I was angry that none of my older siblings had thought to tell Julie we had been left on our own. I felt my usual hatred for Carol, for only ever thinking of herself, and cursed our mother for leaving us. All these thoughts were swirling around my brain as I slowly paced myself to Simon's tiny steps, I didn't care much about anything anymore. The three little ones pestered me for food but I didn't feel hungry and the thought of foraging no longer seemed important. Food had been plentiful whilst the fair had been in town so the need to search, beg and steal to feed ourselves, became too difficult for me to accept.

My survival instincts had relaxed and I wasn't sure if I could do it any more. My mind drifted back just for a few seconds, remembering how it had been when Mother had still been at home - the untidy mess and the bedlam of our uncontrolled siblings all fighting for a piece of what was theirs. The poverty and cruel abuse all ran through my mind creating a sudden surge of fear that shot from my head to my toes.

Then I suddenly realised that maybe what we had was far better than what we had back then. My sudden understanding of Mother's repeated quotation that God works in mysterious ways became my reasoning for being between the devil and the deep blue sea. Up until then I hadn't been able to understand why I'd been left carrying all the responsibility of my three younger siblings on my shoulders, but then suddenly just for a moment I realized it was an honour for me to take care of them. I had previously been taught that God only helps those that helped themselves, so maybe it was having faith in that quotation that gave me the strength to carry on. I stood tall and led my family home happy in the thought that not only had I helped myself but my siblings too.

By the time we arrived home it was dark and Sunday was nearly over. It had been a strange kind of day with very little time to think. Our house was cold and empty and I was feeling lonely but something told me this was the way it was meant to be. There were times when I didn't understand all my thoughts and feelings but even so, I knew the path I was on was the right one.

David and Trevor came home from the farm that night, carrying the strong smell of manure on their Wellington boots. Andrew and I had not felt tired so played with the fire instead. We stripped inner pages from books that we found and threw them into the fireplace to watch them burn. For a short while, with each book we destroyed, we felt the warmth and glow of a fire upon our faces but once our matches had run out and the fire had died down it was bitterly cold again.

David brought back his usual supply of potatoes and a large pack of lard to fry chips. I hated peeling potatoes from the farm, they were so large I could barely hold them in my hands. Some of them were covered in so much mud I couldn't get my knife through them but it was the same for all of us. If we wanted to eat, we had to do the things we disliked doing. I was quicker peeling them than anyone else and didn't complain much, so David gave the job straight to me. I told David we hadn't eaten today so he went upstairs to fetch Lorraine and Simon down but they were so tired they were in too deep a sleep.

When David came back downstairs, he came towards me and took two of the largest potatoes out of the sink and placed them on the draining board. *"Cook um some chips tomorrow, Molly and don' waste the gas,"* he said. I knew, and I think David knew, that the potatoes he had put aside would not only feed Lorraine and Simon tomorrow but Andrew and I as well. We shared everything. Sometimes survival was an unfair game; but who was judging?

After supper Andrew and I went upstairs to bed, soon after I heard David and Trevor going to their room at the back of the house, climbing into their rickety bunk beds. I seemed to sleep easier when they were at home, I had never liked it in the house on my own. I was frightened of everything, the dark peering through the windows, the open loft and the untidy bathroom and yet, at times when I'd been left alone, I'd faced my fears full on with that strange inner strength that we all seem to have at times, sometimes creating the ability to cast all my fears aside. As I lay quietly on my bed listening to David and Trevor settling into theirs, my thoughts drifted to Mother, as I closed my eyes and went to sleep.

—〰—

CHAPTER 11

My Worst Nightmare

During the following weeks things changed, but not the way I had hoped.

It was a normal day for us, David and Trevor went off to the farm like they usually did while my younger siblings and I roamed the streets, scavenging food from neighbours' dustbins. We were in our element rummaging through them, occasionally cutting our fingers on the sharp edges of discarded cans and broken bottles but blood trickling down our fingers had never deterred us before. So we spent our days in other peoples' back yards searching through bins picking out food and anything we thought may be of some use, occasionally we were chased up garden paths but it was a risk we took when we needed to eat. We had returned to our old ways and again had become self-sufficient; since the fair had left the whole of that day had been pretty much like any other. Food, as usual, was our main priority and as the day came to an end and night began to fall we ate what we had found, then we took ourselves off to bed.

We had been in bed for quite a while before I heard David and Trevor come thundering through our front door, behaving recklessly and very irresponsibly. Having spent a lot of time with them since we had been abandoned I recognised something unusual, a difference in their behaviour. They were singing and shouting, swearing and cursing, making me feel very apprehensive. It was so unlike them, my curiosity got the better of me so I climbed out of bed and crept downstairs. I walked across the hall to where the shouting came from, and noticing the kitchen door slightly ajar I risked my hide to find out what all the noise was about. I walked towards the kitchen door careful not to make a sound and turned my ear towards the kitchen, listening for a while. Suddenly I was aware of a third voice echoing through our house, a voice that caused my skin to crawl and my heart to pound. I trembled as the very distinctive husky voice penetrated my ears. Suddenly I felt the urge to urinate as a fear inside me built to an uncontrollable height forcing the fluid from my body with a strength and determination. As I stood in a large pool of urine, I reached for the door handle preparing myself for my worst nightmare. Timidly I opened the door, stood and observed then froze as I came face to face with our brother John. My entire thoughts, my whole mind blanked with fear.

I stood in the doorway trembling as my brothers' voices fell silent. He sat on the kitchen chair looking straight at me, his eyes like daggers, but he said nothing, he almost looked as shocked as I felt. He raised his right hand and took a large gulp from the bottle of beer he held in his fist. His eyes full of hate he slammed it back down onto the kitchen table, stood up and walked towards me. He was much larger than I had remembered and more frightening by far.

I was stunned when he leaned forward and with just one grasp of his fist around the bodice of my dress he forcibly swept me off my feet, muttering in his unpleasant manner, *"Well look who we have here"*.

For that moment my thoughts were completely lost to him. I felt sick as I took in the whole picture of David and Trevor celebrating his return with bottles upon bottles of stout and nut brown. I felt hurt and betrayed and at that moment I felt more of an outsider than I ever had. John fell back onto the chair as he lost his balance still holding me tight within his grasp, he exaggerated his usual sick abusive laugh as I fell onto his knee. I held myself rigid with fear as he got up from the chair and stood to attention. Placing his hands under my armpits, he lifted me and held me high in the air for several minutes whilst he displayed his usual show of strength, then without warning he dropped me to the floor. My feet hit the quarry tiles hard sending ripples of pain through my feet up to my stomach. With tears rolling down my cheeks, I plucked up enough courage to ask if I could go back to bed but he ignored me, leaving me to fret for a while. I stood in the middle of the kitchen with my chin on my chest and tears dripping onto the floor. Crying silently, remembering how it angered him to hear me snivel, I flinched with every movement he made and trembled as he moved towards his chair. A whole lifetime of abusive memories ran through my mind as I unwillingly recalled the occasions when he had felt it necessary to hang me upside down through his bedroom window before he raped me a second and third time.

As he casually placed one leg in a kneeling position on top of his seat he leant forward with his face in mine and whispered, *"Now fuck off"* and with the tone of his voice, I knew there was more to come. As I turned away from him I felt a sharp kick to my buttocks, which caused me to jolt and cry out as I shunted forward and lost my balance. My hands shot out in front of me to save myself from falling as I landed hard, hitting the door frame. I moved quickly and ran upstairs to bed, desperately hoping he wouldn't follow me. Climbing into the bed I had been sleeping in for some time I snuggled up to my siblings, hoping in some way they would protect me.

It was a while before I heard someone creep upstairs and go to the bathroom, I listened to every movement they made and heard them flush the toilet and sneak into our room. I was too frightened to open my eyes. I knew it was him, I could hear the same heavy breathing that I had heard many times before but I kept my eyes tightly closed and pretended to be asleep, hoping he would go away, but I was wrong. He crept to the side of our bed and without a second's thought he lifted me quietly from it so as not to disturb my younger siblings. He tucked me into his arms and carried me to the single bed that was still at the foot of the large bed. I trembled with fear, determined not to cry as he stood silent for a while, looking down on me. I felt his hot breath on my face as he held me motionless above the single bed, then suddenly his arms opened and I fell, and responding to the sudden fall I put out my arms to stop myself from falling and landed hard onto the bed. When I opened my eyes and looked up, he was leaning forward and frowning, and without showing any emotion he ordered me to sleep there.

He had changed in the years since I had seen him, his eyes were more piercing and his face more solemn but the harshness in his voice was much the same as it had always been. He walked out of our room and into the boys' room, then, returned with a blanket to cover me.

I felt cold and nervously flinched as he leaned over my bed, tucking the blanket around me. Loathing every minute of it I reluctantly listened as he whispered a few kind words in that strange tone of voice that told me I still couldn't trust him.

Since I last saw him I had grown a little and changed no doubt, but within a few minutes of seeing him I was reminded of his cruel actions, of the crazy and neurotic personality with which he had managed to instill all the fear I had of him before he went away.

I feared him more than anything and hadn't been able to forget all the cruel things he had done to me; the repeated threats, the blood, pain and all the fear he had caused me. I had not forgotten all the nights that led up to him taking away my innocence and even after all those years I still recalled what it had been like to fear for my life.

I had discovered since his return he had started back at the farm with David and Trevor. I seem to remember him constantly talking about June, a girl he knew up there. He wanted everyone to know that she was his girl-friend and he boasted of sexual activities that took place between them. I only ever recall seeing her the once but heard him say many times she was the farmer's daughter, he saw her most days yet his routine of molesting me didn't seem to change. He still came home late at night and woke me from my sleep and David, who remained ignorant to the fact of his behaviour, still dragged me out of bed in order to cook their suppers.

Despite John's disruptive influence things seemed to run quite smoothly for a while. He moved in to our house like he had never been away, causing very little pain and suffering to any of the others, but he couldn't help the occasional bang of his fist around my head and kick to my buttocks that he found rather amusing, but on the whole things remained quite calm.

He had only been home for a few days when out of the blue, Carol sprung a visit. She came during the day when John, David and Trevor were at the farm and asked me lots of questions, some I didn't know the answer to and others I didn't understand. How long had he been home? Where was he sleeping? And how long was he staying for? She sounded concerned, although I couldn't believe it was for me! I didn't want to believe it was for him either! I thought maybe she was looking forward to seeing him after all the years he had been away, but I remained a little sceptical. Carol wasn't an easy person to understand, I never knew what she was really thinking. While she waited she cleaned a little and washed what few bits of crockery we had left, swept and mopped the floors, then, burnt lots of old papers we had thoughtlessly scattered around the house, then folded some of the larger sized clothing we had tried for size whilst searching for something to wear.

It was nightfall before our house was moderately clean. She explained she'd be staying the night and she would be sleeping with me. I was pleased and smiled at her with a look of appreciation. I was sure she was staying to protect me from him yet she never mentioned a word about him abusing me. For the first time since he had been home, I felt in safe hands. As Carol spoke, she mentioned Father a few times giving me the impression she had seen him and he was going to visit. I tried to get my head around everything that was happening but one thing I had never been able to understand was why, when John was taken away, did most of my family leave too?

Now he was back, it seemed they were slowly coming back. I had always thought I was to blame for John being taken away and always associated us being left on our own because of me, but now I wasn't so sure.

The whole day felt quite strange. Carol hadn't shouted or punched me once and just so she could feed us she walked us all across to the Co-op to see Frank herself instead of sending me like she usually did, and asked him for a tin of baked beans and a loaf of bread until tomorrow, when she said she would pay him. He obliged and this seemed to put her into an even better mood. She seemed different somehow, as if she was only following someone's instructions, yet, she knew exactly what she was doing.

After giving us supper, she tucked us up into bed and gave us all a kiss, then for the first time in a long time she sat on our bed singing to us just like she used to. It was something she had done almost every night when our parents had been together. I chose songs for her to sing, although 'Marianna' was her favourite and always sung first, mine was 'Santa Lucia' and was sung afterwards. She went through a whole range of songs including 'Ave Maria', trying to encourage me to sleep, but it all felt so special she fell asleep well before I did. I once heard Mother say "music soothes the savage breast". She was right; Carol slept like a baby at the side of me, her head resting on my chest and as quiet as a lamb.

Carol made a big difference to that day and although I sensed she knew something I didn't, I made the most of her unusual kindness and her willingness to clean the house. I wondered at some point if Mother was coming home, or perhaps Miss Woodward was calling? I knew there was something, but Carol kept her secret close to her heart. The only thing she made clear to me was that she wouldn't be staying after tomorrow and I'd have to take good care of myself. She said she was returning to the Dunns in Staveley but at that moment in time it didn't worry me for I had learned never to think of tomorrow and only the day we were living was important. There were a few things I vowed I would never do again, one was to trust and the other was to let go of something that was mine. I knew I had to forget the days that had long since passed and keep my head and thoughts clear but most of all I had to live for the present.

I had already lost the trust I once had in my family and assumed that whatever they did now, they did for themselves. Carol, however, did as she promised that night; she stayed at our house and slept with me in my bed. When I awoke the following morning she was up and already downstairs. As I made my own way down I could hear her in the kitchen talking to someone, and when I reached the kitchen door I was surprised to see it was John. It was unusual for him not to go to the farm with David and Trevor, so I wondered why he hadn't. I began to think all kinds of things, especially as Carol had said she was leaving that day. I tried not to show John I was frightened of him, but I'm sure he sensed my fear as I moved nervously around the kitchen trying to avoid him.

Carol still didn't seem herself, she flinched as John walked by her and seemed more on edge than usual. She stood resting her back on the kitchen sink, staring into thin air, chewing on her finger nails, taking particular notice of John's movements as he stalked the house and lit up one cigarette after another, puffing at each one as it if were his last. Andrew and Lorraine where already out of the house, digging the garden with Mother's spoons and raking up the damp soil in front of the kitchen window. Simon was now able to sit in his pram as Carol had spent time cleaning it with bleach and disinfectant that she had brought with her. It was the first time it had been cleaned since Mother had left, so it was unusual to see him sitting in there.

Seeking protection from John, I shuffled slowly towards Carol and stood at her side. I had a strange feeling we were waiting for something to happen. They were silent, just waiting and listening. As time went by John became agitated and moved into the front room. I could hear his footsteps as he paced the length of the room, back and forth, repeating his steps over and over again. Carol, still chewing on her finger nails, remained fixed to the kitchen sink while I had now reluctantly claimed the kitchen chair in which John had been sitting. I stripped off lengths of newspaper and rolled them in between my fingers to make paper sticks, for the lighting of the fire. John left a few old newspapers on the hearth ready for making a fire but he never bought wood or coal to go with them, just as he had never supplied Mother with any money towards his upkeep. John was thoroughly selfish. Even if he was cold and hungry and had money enough to buy food and coal, he never would, if it meant we would have benefited from it too. He had been this way as far back as I could remember and because of his mad, violent temper, we all accepted it.

For a few minutes, our house was peaceful. John had stopped pacing the floor and Simon was asleep in his pram, Carol and I were in the kitchen keeping our heads down. Whenever John was around our house was at its quietest, no one dared make a sound - even our dog Kim remained under the kitchen table until he was out of sight. Suddenly with a bark that startled us all, Kim ran from under the table and through the open door as fast as he could. He had heard footsteps at the top of our path and barked excitedly; it wasn't his usual protective bark, so, we all knew the visitor we had was no stranger.

John was the first to respond. He ran through the dining room and out of the back door knocking the kitchen table clear across the room. It was obviously what he'd been waiting for. His face was red with anger and his actions told me it was a fight he was looking for. He was always fighting with someone from our neighbourhood and enjoyed the thrill of it all.

He was proud when his opponent begged him for mercy but I took no pleasure in watching him fight. I knew the crowds gave him strength and encouragement but I prayed that one day he would meet his match. Within minutes of John going through the door, it was obvious a fight was in progress. I listened to the usual crowds shouting and screaming but suddenly, noticed this time it was different. The worried spectators screamed for him to stop and informed him with loud, frightened voices that he would kill him if he didn't. Out of curiosity, I leaned my head around the doorjamb to find the fight was situated in the middle of our garden path, with no access around it. The crowds had gathered all around John and his victim, who by now was lying between the coal shed and our house with his legs trapped between the two. I couldn't get to see who he was so I ran to our front door and flung it wide open, looking for any signs.

At first I couldn't take it in, but then I recognised Father's car at the front of our house, and suddenly it gave me the most sickening feeling within my stomach, as I realised John, my brother, my abuser, was beating up my father.

There was blood everywhere. My father's hands where resting flat on the ground at the side of him and folk were supporting his weak and battered body. My hysterical screams didn't deter John and he continued to punch Father's face over and over again trying his damndest to kill him. As I ran through our house to the back yard, I grabbed Father's axe off the trestle and ran to the front with it. I wanted to kill John myself, I'd hated him for so long but now I really wanted to kill him.

The crowd tried to persuade him to calm down but he was so angry he slammed one punch after another into Father's face. I saw Father propped up against the coal-house door, helpless and weak with blood streaming from his nose, turning his cream coloured shirt into a blood stained rag. Father's ear was cut and bleeding with traces of blood running down his cheek, he was covered in so much blood yet as he looked up at me, I could still see the tears in his eyes. That day I cried for Father and for myself wondering what it was that we had done to deserve all this.

Father tried to protect his face from more of John's violent punches, but without success. My siblings where screaming hysterically and I tried to get close to my father, begging John to stop, but the more I pleaded with him the more he punched. He was furious and well out of control, no better than a rabid animal. Father had gashes and cuts on the backs of his hands where John had been kicking him. Finally John ran out of breath and as he stood in silence, shaking with temper the crowd tried to persuade him to walk away.

Our neighbour offered him a few cigarettes to leave Father alone, and although he was reluctant, the mention of the police seem to finalise things and he walked away leaving Father wedged between our house and the coal shed, crying and trembling with so much fear that he couldn't move.

A few good men came to Father's aid and helped him to his feet before Carol was able to guide him into our house to clean his wounds. It was the saddest day of my life. I cried more for my father than I did for myself – that was a day I will never ever forget.

John regretted serving four years of his life in prison for sexually abusing me. The beating I witnessed was his revenge on Father for reporting him. Although Carol had been the one to recognise the sign of abuse, Father was the brave man who brought it to the attention of the police. That day he received the beating of his life for protecting me, but in my eyes he still remained the stronger character of the two, as it took more strength to recognise his son's disrespect for his baby sister than it did for John to beat an old man.

John never did accept responsibility for his own actions and found it impossible to accept that what he did to me was wrong. I remember I once prayed for a member of my family to come home and help me with my younger siblings, but never once did I imagine it would be him. I regretted that prayer so often and wondered – if there really was a God, why did He send him?

I heard Carol talking to Father in the kitchen while she cleaned up his face. The conversation was to do with getting help for us children. I didn't understand much, but I was aware of the talk about us going away. It didn't worry me, I really hoped we would but I had long since learned to hide my feelings, that way I never hurt anyone. I knew I would do better if I left home but I wasn't so sure about my siblings. Mother had often used it as a threat before she left and often made them cry, so, I wasn't sure they'd be happy.

Father knew he couldn't leave me alone with John in the house, so he asked Carol to stay just until he could sort something out. She promised faithfully she would, but she changed her mind so often, her word was unreliable. As John came into the house, Father nervously picked up his jacket from the back of the chair and asked Carol to help him put it on. He walked towards the front door and bent down to kiss me on my cheek. His lips where still bleeding and I could smell the Germoline that Carol had smeared on the swollen parts of his cheeks. His tears were now fixed to the inner corners of his eyes looking like they were made of glass and I had to hold tight to the very large lump that had formed in the back of my throat, just to stop myself from crying.

I felt for my father as he walked up the garden path on his own. I really wished it was John who was leaving, he didn't belong here, he never did. He was cruel, offensive and really hated being with us, so I wondered why he stayed.

Father drove away in his car trying to raise a smile, but, he couldn't hide the hurt he felt inside. He had grown old, his hair was white and he was fragile. His appearance had always been the same, yet my heart went out to him each time I saw him. He was a lovely man and didn't deserve to be treated the way John treated him, just as John didn't deserve to have a father as kind as him.

Once he had left, Carol and I walked back into the house and cried silently. It had been a long time since I had seen her cry, but today her tears ran as freely down her cheeks as mine did.

John was standing with his back to the kitchen sink. He was quiet, but still looked angry. His hands shook violently as he held a cigarette to his mouth. Taking long drawn out breaths of smoke to the back of his throat, he forced it out in huge puffs as he glared first at Carol, then at me. It was that awful look that made me realise he hadn't changed, in fact I think being in prison had made him worse.

Carol had sent our younger siblings upstairs out of his way knowing they were safer there, since his unwarranted attack on Father she had become a little more protective. They were quiet so it may have been possible that they had fallen to sleep. This gave her time to write a list for me to take over the road to Frank. Father had given Carol two notes, one to pay Frank for the food we had on tick and the other for food we needed now. It wasn't much but it was all he had. Having written the list, Carol rolled up the notes and wrapped them securely in the tatty paper she had written it on and handed me Mother's large shopping bag from the pantry. She sent me on my way with the parcel of notes firmly pressed to my palm and securely wrapped in my fist, giving me strict orders not to lose it. I took the bag and note across to Frank and watched him open it, he was a little apprehensive but then his eyebrows lifted and he raised a smile as he proceeded to collect items of food from the shelves. He added up the price of each item on his note pad that lay on the counter in front of him then placed all the items in my bag. Dropping a little change into one of the side pockets he smiled again and said, " *There you go Molly,*" as he reached above my head and opened the shop door, allowing me to walk through it. I struggled with the heavy load, holding the handles with both hands until Carol caught a glimpse of me, then she grabbed the bag with one hand and lifted it up onto our kitchen table where she unloaded the contents and placed them on to the pantry shelves.

Andrew, Lorraine and Simon had woken up and were playing in the dining room. Everyone seemed relaxed, and I scanned the room wondering where John was, then Carol smiled and told me he had gone to work. He was the farmer's main worker so was allowed to go in late, so long as he made up the time.

After giving us all something to eat, Carol explained she would have to collect some of her clothes from the Dunns if she was going to stay with us for a while, but promised faithfully to be on the last bus back home. But I knew her better than most and realised her word wasn't good. She never did make that last bus back. I wasn't surprised, I knew before she left that she wasn't coming home.

That night I went to bed crying. There was nothing worse than wanting someone to come home and then they didn't. She had left me open to John's cruelty and abuse and I was terrified. It was usually when he returned from the farm at night that he was at his worst; and she knew that. The fear of him coming back made me tremble.

I pulled up the only blanket on my bed to cover my face hoping somehow it would protect me. I had already dismissed the thought of walking all the way to Stavely with my younger siblings as Carol wasn't the most considerate person and wouldn't have thought twice about sending us back home, even in the dark.

Although I felt a little protected having David and Trevor around, I knew they were no match for John, and I cried when I realised there was no escape for me. It had been a long time since Mother had left and our little family had come through so much together, but my heart sank as I realised how my life was going to be from now on. I had spent so much time looking after the others my only wish was to have someone to look after me. I couldn't remember the last time I wore clean clothes, took a nice warm bath or even felt thoroughly safe. Even our hairbrush would no longer go through my hair. I had outgrown my shoes and walked bare-foot. This was my life, my home - how I wished I could have changed it.

That night I dreamt I wore clean clothes and walked in red patent shoes, but as I desperately tried to hold onto my dream, I was awakened by the familiar feeling of someone touching me. It took me a while to realise what was happening, but it soon became apparent that, that terrible sensation was for real. It had been years since I had last experienced it and as the chafing got worse my tears ran freely from the corners of my eyes. I realised the sexual abuse I once had to put up with, had now begun again. As I felt my vagina being prized apart I lay on my bed just wishing with all my heart, I could die. As John inserted his fingers, I felt pain like I had never felt before. Trying hard to pull away, I hoped he would leave my room but he looked at me with so much hatred in his eyes. I knew this time it would be worse than the last.

I gave out such a cry as his fingers stiffened and the force behind his movements became fast and furious. In an attempt to silence me he pressed his other hand firmly across my mouth and took my breath away. I gasped for breath as he forced his fingers inside my vagina, causing my skin to tear. I struggled to free myself, but he used the whole weight of his body to hold me down, while he molested me. I had forgotten how painful it was to be handled this way and continually pulled away from him. But he was strong and lifted me briskly from my bed and carried me to the bathroom. He stood me down on the floor, while he turned to lock the door and fastened me inside. Wasting no time, he pulled off his trousers and left them crumpled on the floor.

I thought the sound of my continuous crying would have deterred him but, he was as hard as nails, he spared no thought or feeling for anyone. He had the instincts of a savage. It had been years since I last experienced his cruel attacks and had prayed in hope of it never happening again, but here I stood before him, helpless and alone, knowing the abuse I was about to suffer was going to be the worst I had ever had. He grabbed my hand and placed it around his penis ordering me to grip it tight as he demonstrated the rhythm he preferred and I rubbed it like he said to save myself a beating.

One thing I hadn't forgotten was how handy he was with his fist. He forced me to catch his sperm in my mouth as he firmly placed his hands around the back of my head, directing my mouth towards his fully erect penis. In the past he had forced me into doing this so many times it had almost become second nature and although I hated doing it, I preferred to do that rather than what I knew was routinely coming next. It seemed I was rubbing his penis forever before his body shook spasmodically, then he quickly grabbed my head with both hands and pumped his sperm to the back of my throat, allowing time enough for me to swallow before he released me from his grip. I cried as I involuntarily swallowed a mouthful of his sperm, and trying hard not to vomit I tried to rid the horrible sensation it left upon my tongue.

He sat back on the toilet seat and rested for a while, ordering me to stand in front of him, silent and perfectly still. Fumbling with his trousers he dug into his pockets pulling out a small packet of cigarettes and a box of Captain Webb matches. Opening the cigarette packet he pulled out a cigarette and loosely rested it between his lips, then lit it with a match he took from the box. Drawing large breaths of smoke to the back of his throat, he swallowed, then, released it with a deep sigh of contentment.

For a considerable amount of time he ignored me and I began to fall asleep resting on the side of the bath. Finally I built up enough courage to ask if I could go back to bed, but he glared at me with so much hate in his eyes, he almost looked insane. After a short time he knelt down in front of me, with both hands pressed firmly between my legs, he prized them apart and licked repulsively at my flesh. It was only now I dared look down on him with so much hate, I hoped he would die. All the years he had spent away from home, yet he had not learnt. However, I had learnt that what he had done to me most of my life, was unnatural.

As I blanked his present activity, I experienced mixed emotions and shamefully realised my so-called brother was yet again molesting me, damaging what little life I had left.

I was only nine years old, yet fully aware there was no going back. I had learned every sexual organ and the way it functioned before I had reached the age of five. At the age of nine I knew as much about life as any mature woman and carried as much knowledge of copulation as any other person in the world. It had been this way from as far back as I could remember and although I hated him for what he had done, I felt he owned me, mind, body and soul.

His sudden movements brought my attention back to the present. I focused on his hard, callous face as he looked up at me and grinned, giving me a sick, satisfying glare. I knew this look, the strange blaze in his eyes meant he liked what he was doing and wanted more. Resting his large, filthy hands on the side of the bath he pulled himself up onto his feet and began to manipulate his own testicles. He moved slowly towards me, grabbed my hand and forced it back onto his penis, by which time I knew what I was expected to do and did it without thought or feeling. His penis grew and stood erect, and giving it a slightly more violent rub himself, he lifted me up and ordered me to wrap my arms around his neck as he forced my legs around his waist. He positioned me to gain access to my vagina, and pulling my flesh apart; he forced his penis inside me. I cried out in pain, hoping someone would hear me, but the threat of his fist in my face gained my silence. Once again I held on to my cries as my tears ran freely down my cheeks, while yet again he raped me.

My body fell limp as his surged with excitement and I felt the pain as blood trickled from my torn flesh. As he released his sperm into my vagina he took one deep breath and fell silent, savouring that moment like he had no more time to live. I felt his heavy, stinking breath on my face as he yearned for more, but taking no particular notice of the damage he had caused me, he ordered me back to bed.

I knew he hadn't carried out his full routine, I remembered from all those years ago; there was more. He opened the bathroom door and forced me through it ordering me to get into bed, but demand I stay awake. I was hurting and so tired all I wanted to do was sleep, physically and emotionally I was drained. I climbed onto my bed, being careful not to hurt myself even more and sobbed knowing there was no one to protect me. I pulled my blanket over my head and hid away from him, hoping he would forget me.

The warmth and comfort of my own bed helped me to relax as I lay quietly, fighting sleep, but my heart was pounding as I heard him stalking the house just like he used to. My siblings were asleep, while I lay awake, suffering, wondering like so many times before, why me?

Knowing I had no way to escape him, in my childlike way, I placed my hands together, closed my eyes and prayed, and trusting there really was a God, I asked him to save me. This is my prayer as I remember it;

Where do you come from? I am so unsure
My eyes do not see you, but do you see me, Lord?
I do not understand, my mind will not accept
My family has forsaken me, and they have no regrets.
I have no friends, yet I yearn for many.
Pray Lord who will love one so melancholy,
Whose heart breaks, whose tears flow
I know not real love, how can that be so?

I am here Lord, all alone, can you not see?
There is nothing left on this earth, for a little girl like me.
How will I know you when you come to take my hand?
Will you ease away my pain, hold me close and comfort me?
In this cruel world I see little hope for me;
An innocent child; Suffering miserably!

I spoke of my terrible pain and misery and begged him
over and over again, if he couldn't save me, to allow me
to die. Although I hadn't ever thought of leaving my
younger siblings before, I thought they were more likely
to survive than I was. As my body relaxed and my eyes
closed, I fell asleep hoping I wouldn't wake up.

—⁓—

CHAPTER 12

My Prayers are Answered

I must have slept for some time before I felt John roughly shaking me, he whispered my name so as not to wake my siblings. I was desperately tired and found it easy to ignore him until he began prodding me, insisting that I move. It was the firm demand of his angry voice that frightened me. I covered my face with both hands, too ashamed to cry but he did no more than turn away and walk to the bathroom knowing I would follow him; I was too frightened not to. As I climbed down from my bed I felt a heavy throbbing pain surge from my stomach to my vagina, I was so sore I was terrified of it all happening again. I hobbled back to the bathroom, where he stood waiting for me. With the slightest click of his fingers I remembered the exact routine and curved my body over the side of the bath trying to support myself, as he ordered me to stay still. Moving swiftly, he removed his trousers and straddled around me, forcing his hands beneath my stomach, he lifted my bottom so high that it enabled him to stroke his penis around the aperture of my anus, gradually forcing it into my anal passage. It caused me so much pain I jumped and tried to pull away, and expressing how much it hurt, I begged him to stop, but he thrived on my suffering. A look of anger spread over his face as he grabbed a large fist full of my hair and yanked my head, before making his usual abusive threats. Then he forced my body back over the side of the bath as his strong desire to molest me took full hold of him. Like a man possessed he roughly guided his penis back into my anal passage, placed both hands under my stomach and pulled me up towards him. I couldn't stop crying, but I tried to keep my whimpering to a minimum so as not to wake my siblings. As the severity of his attack overwhelmed me, I suffered a sudden fit of hysteria which gave him all the excitement he required to obtain that one final burst of satisfaction. I cried out for my Mother as he thrust with all his might, but ignoring my cries, he broke me.

My feeble body hung motionless over the side of the bath as his penis pulsated inside me. Showing no mercy, he relaxed in silence as his heavy panting became the ghastly sound that has gone on to haunt me all my life.

That night my prayers were answered when a sudden look of horror spread over his face and the silence in our house was broken The house echoed to a loud, forceful knocking at our front door which filled our home and finally gave me a feeling of hope. The high pitch barking from Kim woke my siblings as he rushed around our house, alerting us of strangers.

David and Trevor panicked as they woke and called out to John as they made their way downstairs, and ordering Kim to be silent David called John's name again. His voice registered urgency, encouraging John to pull away from me. I remained curved over the side of the bath, waiting nervously for him to dismiss me.

At the sudden click of his fingers I stood to attention, by which time he was struggling to put on his trousers. The fear of getting caught panicked him, his balance was affected, he became hot and flustered and for the first time in his life that I could remember, he looked scared. He ordered me to wait in the bathroom until he came back. Although I was frightened, I knew at least for now my painful ordeal was over. He opened the bathroom door, ran through it and slammed it shut behind him.

I cried the moment he left the bathroom, and feeling an urgent need to open my bowels, I climbed onto the toilet but apart from the blood- stained sperm that ran freely from my orifices, I achieved nothing. The severity of pain around my stomach had subsided but the soreness and heavy throbbing from my torn flesh was agonising. Inquisitively I tried to check the damage he had caused me, but the slightest touch made it impossible. I lowered myself down from the toilet and turned on the cold water tap, grabbed a towel from the large pile of dirty laundry that lay on the floor and wet a small corner of it. Cautiously, I dabbed at my vagina with the cool wet corner, wincing, as I tried to ease my pain.

I pulled down and straightened my dress as I walked over to the bathroom door. Opening it slightly I could hear the voices downstairs. I heard someone ask John if they could come inside but he immediately refused them entry. They asked him many questions, some relating to Andrew, Lorraine and myself but he was very deceptive. They made a point of asking to see Mr Wass but he informed them, he was Mr Wass. They were obviously losing patience with him and made it blatantly clear they needed to see our parents, but he ignored every request they made, repeatedly asking who they were and what they wanted. They were very evasive and John was rude and argued with them for some time, making it clear he wouldn't allow them across the threshold until he knew exactly who they were. I sensed the nervousness in his voice as he tried to keep them away, but suddenly he lost all authority when the familiar voice of our local policeman, Mr Sergeant, became firm and distinctive and without hesitation John allowed him through the front door. Within a few moments our house was swarming with people, all searching for my siblings and myself.

I sniggered to myself; suddenly realising even John had a fear of certain people. He hated not being in command and tonight was one of those very few times when he lost his control over us. He remained aggressive and refused point blank to allow them upstairs, eventually they agreed that he could bring us down. Knowing him well, Mr Sergeant instructed him to remain calm and advised him to co-operate with the social workers. John hesitated for a while, then with a slight quiver in his voice, he replied, in the most nonchalant manner, *"Yes, officer"*.

He moved like a flash of lightning and I jumped back as he kicked open the bathroom door. Grabbing hold of my arm, he dragged me into the bedroom showing nothing but anger as he raised his hand in the way of a threat. I flinched as I rather expected him to give me a back hander like he always did but that night it was different, he knelt down in front of me and glared straight into my eyes as he forced my head up by placing his index finger under my chin. With his face only inches away from mine, he sneered as he acknowledged

LITTLE MOLLY

the fear I had of him and gave me one last warning to say absolutely nothing about the sadistic abuse he inflicted on me. As the memories of him hanging me upside down through his bedroom window flashed through my mind, I recalled his violent attack on my father, and nervously nodded to everything he said. He grabbed my arms and shook me violently to affirm his warning, then threw me to the floor.

Shaking nervously, I remained on the floor as I watched him uncover Andrew and Lorraine. Ordering them downstairs, he reached for Simon and swiftly picked him up, chucked him to one side and wrapped his left arm around his middle as if he were a sack a spuds, then walked through the bedroom door and downstairs with me following him.

By the time we had reached the bottom step, we had been taken aside and each one of us handed over to a stranger, wrapped up with larger sized clothing from the kitchen and escorted to a car that was parked at the front of our house. Everything happened so fast that I lost track of my thoughts and stood back to take stock of what was happening. The social workers didn't seem very tactful or friendly, I almost feared them as much as I feared John, yet I still went with them. I knew they were people with authority but I wasn't sure that I could trust them. I hoped with all my heart that whatever it was they had planned for us, it would be better than the life we had had so far.

One of them opened the car door and stood back while my siblings and I climbed into the back seat. I comforted them as they cried out for Mother and gently rocked Simon in my arms as the car pulled away from our house. I looked around and I remember

seeing Trevor screaming as he fought off the other
two strangers. He wasn't quite as tall as David but having worked on Ward's farm he was almost as strong.
He was only aged ten but he held tight to the door
jamb screaming for help, the only wish he had was to
remain at home. I saw the strength of his grip and the
sadness in his eyes as tears rolled down his cheeks
and he broke down and cried. No matter how much
I tried I could not understand what life at home had
been like for Trevor or my siblings, I only knew what
happened to me made me hate it. They knew nothing
of my abuse, I'm sure of that now. My life had never
been like theirs.

They had been part of each other and shared everything, but I was a loner, I felt alone. I had nothing to
share only deep, damaging thoughts of perverted sexual
abuse and because of that, I was close to no one. As the
car pulled further away from our house, we left Trevor
standing in the distance, and I cried at the thought of
never seeing him again. Then my thoughts turned to my
older siblings; I wasn't going to miss them.

By the time I had reached the age of four, I had
suffered so many beatings and experienced so much
sexual abuse that I suffered from an enormous fear of
human contact. In a period of six years among a family of twelve only the abusers themselves were aware
of my constant pain and suffering. The other siblings,
my father and my mother knew nothing until it was
too late, and even then they found it difficult to accept
that it all happened in and around the house where
they lived.

I had never imagined that it could have ended this
way. Had I realised my siblings were happy to stay at

home I wouldn't have included them in my prayers for help. I myself was grateful to our social worker Miss Woodward, for her insight, and to the Derbyshire County Council's team who gave me a chance to live my life as a normal child. In the weeks, months and years to come I tried to forget my life of pain and misery and tried to look forward to a life with new hopes and new beginnings; something I had always dreamt about.

—◊—

CHAPTER 13

Our New Beginning

The long journey through that night was one that I have always been able to remember. Although I wasn't sure where we were heading I knew this was it, my chance to break from the past, from all the hard times and bitter memories, from that place I had called home. We were now leaving everything behind and I was moving forward to start a new life.

We had been travelling for hours I'm sure, and although I had slept some of the way I could tell by the changing light it was approaching morning. My siblings were still asleep as the car turned into a large driveway and parked in an area surrounded by yew trees. A large house stood proudly among acres of well-maintained lawns and although it stood in darkness, the bright night sky gave it an eerie silhouette and I couldn't help being frightened of the size and seclusion of the building. I had never seen a house so large and it gave me a sudden feeling of fear for the future. I don't know what it was that I had expected to find at the end of our journey but this wasn't it. I wasn't sure whether part of me was regretting being rescued or if it was my fear of the unknown that was confusing me.

My fear grew stronger as my siblings and I slowly emerged from the car and we were led to a large oak door at the front of the house. Reluctantly we followed the social workers, through the door and into the house where we found a dark and gloomy room, lit with a very small light. As I looked around I noticed a high - backed wooden bench standing in the corner of the room. The walls were made of dark oak panels that stretched all the way through the corridor to the other end of the house and the parquet flooring was highly buffed and covered with an Indian rug that was a little worn in places. But as I looked around, I saw no evidence of children, the place was immaculately clean and I remember a strong smell of furniture polish.

At that moment I became nervous and tears trickled down my cheeks. Although I tried to keep control; my feelings of insecurity and uncertainty were far stronger. Trying to hold back the sudden flow of tears, I swallowed hard as a large lump formed at the back of my throat and I broke down and cried. I shed enough tears that night to last a lifetime. As I tried to dry my tears with the back of my hand, I saw two females coming towards me - one took a peep at Simon, who was still fast asleep in my arms and she shook her head as she peered down at him. I wasn't sure what this gesture meant, but her face was solemn and as she approached the male social worker, she shook her head again and said *"He's beautiful, but far too young to stay here"*. For me that was the biggest shock of all, I broke into hysterics as she tried her best to calm me. She explained he was too young and needed the appropriate care of a nursery, but I couldn't bear to hear it. As she reached out and took him from my arms, it felt like she was tearing my heart apart. He was

18 months old and had been wrapped in my arms for so long, he almost felt a part of me. I couldn't believe they were tearing us apart, surely they knew that all we had was each other! I knew when they walked out of that room with Simon I had lost my baby brother.

That night must have been the longest night of my life. After being scrubbed clean and fitted with pyjamas we were finally tucked into bed, where we slept soundly for hours. The following day I awoke around lunchtime to find Andrew and Lorraine had already gone downstairs to meet the people who were to be our new carers. I reluctantly climbed from my bed and nervously walked to the bathroom, were I met with someone called Auntie Gina. She made it clear I'd be calling all members of staff Auntie and ran through a few of their names. After allowing me to use the bathroom she led me to the store cupboard at the rear of the dormitory, and helped me to choose clothing from the new and used clothing stocks. I couldn't help feeling shy and embarrassed as I tried on various items for size and noticed she did her best to preoccupy herself while I tried on certain garments, and although her presence still made me feel uneasy, her turning away eased my mind a little.

I left the built-in store cupboard alongside Gina with her arm around my shoulders. As we walked to the far end of the dormitory she directed me to a large set of drawers and told me that for the time I was there they were mine. She lifted the large pile of clothing from my arms and placed it neatly into the drawers, keeping back a pleated skirt, jumper and some under garments which she laid neatly on my bed. She smiled as she placed a pair of black, shiny shoes on the floor next to me. Whistling cheerfully, she left the room, leaving me to get dressed.

My new clothes felt rather strange but at the same time made me feel a little bit special. I had a new matching pair of white vest and pants, which felt really soft against my skin and looked rather like the ones I had seen in shop windows in our hometown. My white ankle socks were turned over at the tops and gave my new shoes a very elegant look. By the time I had pulled on my jumper and wrapped the skirt around me, I couldn't help feeling a little stifled and uncomfortable and wondered if this was how Peter and Jane from the Ladybird books had felt when they had new clothes.

I walked through to the bathroom and climbed on to the edge of the bath to view myself in the small mirror above one of the sinks. I couldn't help thinking I looked a little bit funny as the clean and very smart looking Molly peered back at me. She didn't look like me at all.

I jumped down from the bath and walked steadily down the long, wide staircase, being careful not to trip in my new shoes. I glanced down at my feet as I took each step as if it were my first. Although my feet felt clumsy and restricted, I tried to walk with dignity and for the first time in my life, I felt proud to be Molly.

Still feeling nervous and unsure of the place, I stood briefly at the foot of the stairs, taking stock of all the different rooms around the house. I leaned forward and looked to the left. A great white Pyrenean mountain dog laid stretched out the full length of the corridor and allowed a tiny grey terrier to lay at his side, both basking in a ray of sunlight that shone through the open door of a small room to the left of them. I wasn't sure where I was supposed to be but knew full well I wasn't going to attempt to pass by those sleeping dogs. I walked a little to my right, peeping through an open door, where I saw a large yellow-painted room. On the nearside, stood an oblong table set with yellow crockery, for so many people I couldn't count! The room adjacent to it was painted a beautiful red and had the same colour crockery to compliment it. As I made my way slowly to the end of the corridor I glanced through the last open door to see yet another room, painted green. I was amazed by the matching sets of plates, cups and saucers on each table and first thought, I must be dreaming. I closed my eyes and shook my head from side to side, thinking that once I'd re-opened them, everything would have disappeared. But as I slowly opened them, I looked around and realised, this strange and beautiful place was for real.

I felt extremely hungry as the smell of food and cooking, filled the house. Yet the place seemed desolate. I couldn't imagine where the other children were – even Lorraine and Andrew had disappeared. I worried desperately about my younger siblings, and as my imagination ran wild, strange thoughts filled my head. As tears began to roll down my cheeks, the door to my left burst wide open and groups of children of all sizes came tumbling through it. In no time at all, the house was full of children, laughing and shouting, each going their separate ways.

As I quickly tried to wipe away my tears, my siblings stepped through the open doorway with Gina who explained that Andrew and Lorraine had been to visit the school situated on the grounds, and had met their teacher. As she moved closer to me, she let go of my siblings' hands and, with a gentle stroke of her thumb, helped to wipe away my tears. Noticing I flinched, she gently took my hand and led me back down the corridor to the yellow room.

She spoke in an unusually gentle tone that helped me to relax and gave me a feeling of warmth and belonging.

Cradling me on her knee, she explained, the yellow room was our television room, play area and where we had our meals, then went on to say the red and green rooms were reserved for older children. She talked me through a few rules; some I remembered, others just seemed to pass through my brain without registering.

From that day on, each day became a day of learning. We were taught many things, most importantly how to be civilised. We tried to live amongst the other children without fighting, swearing or stealing and although fights broke out, they rarely involved me or my siblings. We began to attend the school, but through lack of space and shortage of staff most age groups were taught together and none of us really progressed in our schooling. Pottery was the main subject taught by Mr Alcock and enjoyed by everyone who lived there. The school had its own firing kiln so we made items we were allowed to keep; this made a huge impact on us all. None of us had any personal belongings so, although many of the items we made were given to visiting relatives, on odd occasions we kept pieces for our own personal use.

My siblings and I soon settled into our new home and although Springhill Children's Home was huge, coming from a large family we soon adjusted to the amount of children living there. Up to thirty children resided at Springhill at any one time. Children were there through similar circumstances to ourselves, following a breakup of their families, victims of abandonment, neglect and abuse, sometimes even children who had been left without any parents at all.

Every child who lived there was anxiously waiting for that special home and family that would be willing to take on our kind. Although Springhill was only a temporary place for children like us, it was our safe haven and while maintaining our stability, it gave us a general insight into what we should expect from a new home and people we lived with. There were no harsh rules there, the staff were kind and easy going, helping me to feel secure and even glad to be alive. Whilst I lived there I was totally free from unnecessary pain, worry and torment. For the first time in my life my thoughts were simple and pure, and although I found it difficult to forget the abuse my brother John inflicted upon me, in time I learned to be "the child that was inside me" and began to place a little trust in the staff who worked there.

I formed a very strong attachment to Gina and in time, she won over my love and entire trust through her natural ability to show love and kindness. She helped me to understand that the feelings we have inside our hearts are a natural force and should be displayed freely, without having to pay a terrible price.

As time passed, I became more confident and grew to have lots of fun. Our daily routine was always the same, school began at 9.30am and I was taught by Mr Allcock just as Gina had promised. He was a kind and pleasant teacher whom I became fond of and purposely stood close to him during lessons. I fought with other children so I could sit next to him and was sure he was everything a father should have been. As my affection for him grew, I sat in class visualizing him as my father. His pleasant features were enlivened by his very kind smile, and his amusing personality won over everyone's trust and earned him the full respect of the class. None of us had attended school much during our past so the work we did was only basic. We were taught from the beginning, starting with our ABCs. Being one of the youngest this didn't seem to bother me but the older children were embarrassed and became angry and frustrated when asked to participate; very often disrupting classes. Although I was able to draw a few simple pictures, I couldn't read or write, not even enough to write my name. But within a few months I had learned to spell and print my own name; Molly, and in time I learned to speak and behave in a more dignified manner and of course, I learned the art of making pottery.

Religious education took place on Sunday mornings at the Sunday school in Duffield. It was a long walk from the house to the main C of E church but after the usual hour-long service I remember Sundays as being very pleasant. During the winter months the long walk was compensated by the beautiful surroundings and my fascination of the long avenue of trees that glistened in the sunshine. The brown, red and gold leaves shimmered through the thick, heavy branches, decorating the pathways with a cascade of colour as their leaves fell in time for autumn. I was enchanted by a magnificent tree house perched high, in one of the trees close to Springhill. A log cabin more beautiful than anything I had ever seen; what a picture of tranquillity and wonder it was to me!

My time at Springhill proved to be one of the happiest times of my life. While I was there I felt, I was the child I was born to be – like a spring lamb being shown the open pastures for the first time. I was playful and amusing and managed to build a screen between the past and the present, allowing my unhappy thoughts and memories to lurk ruthlessly behind a wall of sorrow and hate without it affecting my new beginning.

—ᴡ—

CHAPTER 14

An Unwelcome Change

Springhill became my home, the staff my friends and my life my own and for a while, I was at peace and well protected. But the day came when Gina had to prepare me for a move. I was bewildered and cried all day. Although I still attended school, I was quiet and unco-operative. I sensed Mr Alcock knew I had to leave, some-how he seemed different. Knowing how desperate I was to stay, he looked saddened by it. I wasn't the same in class, I was hurting and although a part of me knew this day would come, I wasn't prepared for it. In the back of my mind, I had always hoped that if I was happy and content, I'd be allowed to stay. I knew nothing of statis-tics back then, but of course, that's all I was – a plain and simple statistic. We were moved, no matter what the outcome!

The following day our transport arrived at midday as arranged and I cried as the car pulled into the driveway. For the first time in a long time I suddenly felt trapped again. I wanted to run and hide so no one could find me but I hadn't the strength to resist the inevitable. Gina looked as sad as I felt - if she hadn't been so strong I'm sure she would have cried as many tears as I did. She always looked a little melancholy on days when children left and her eyes filled with tears as she wrapped her arms around us, giving each of us one last kiss before she led us to the car. Tears trickled down my cheeks as I held tight to her hand, without really understanding why we had to leave. We accepted what we knew was routine and climbed into our new social worker's car. The rest of the children were at school that day so only Gina was there to say goodbye. I wanted to tell her how much I loved her and that I was really going to miss her but I didn't know how, so I left Springhill alongside Andrew and Lorraine, feeling abandoned.

As we began our journey, I sat peering through the rear window, watching all the familiar things disappear out of my life. I never did get to explore the little tree house as I had hoped I would. As we were slowly driven through the beautiful avenue of trees towards the church, we finally passed the large bank that occupied the entire corner of Duffield village; then I knew there was no turning back. My heart sank as I suddenly realised, we were leaving our baby brother behind. I didn't know where he was, but I knew he was staying and we were being driven so far apart, I never expected to see him again. With my child-like thoughts I wondered why God had given him to us in the first place, if he was only going to take him away. I was confused so simply sat and cried.

We travelled for hours without a break, speaking very few words to our new social worker. I blamed her for our unwelcomed move and showed no interest in where we were going and even when she tried to make conversation with me, I paid very little attention to her. I wasn't interested in anything she had to say and felt as if I really hated her, I was unhappy and wanted her to know that.

As my bitter frustration grew, I buried my emotions deep within myself and whispered all the names of people that I knew. I had been let down so many times I had already learned that life didn't always go the way we wanted, but for some reason when I first arrived at Springhill, I had expected permanency. I felt full of sorrow and cried myself to sleep thinking only of the people I had left behind.

When I awoke, our journey was almost over. The avenue of trees on the last stretch of road was similar to the ones that led up to Springhill, except the tiny village was surrounded by large open fields, filled with cattle and flocks of sheep. Our social worker drove steadily up the narrow road trying hard to avoid the large wet cow-pats, until she arrived at a pair of large blue gates firmly attached to an old grey wall. Climbing out of her car, she walked cautiously around it, avoiding the sodden parts of the road and slowly pushed open the gates. As she drove up the driveway, I gazed in admiration at an island out of which a large tree and an assortment of flowers grew; the grounds were truly remarkable.

The house was very large and although it wasn't quite the size of Springhill there was no doubt it was more beautiful. Its large bay windows were dressed with white cotton lace while both sets of French doors had green floral curtains. At the main entrance was a large oak door fitted with a beautiful brass letterbox.

Our social worker carefully parked her car in front of the house, climbed out of her seat and knocked on the front door using the heavy brass knocker, then hurriedly helped all three of us, from the back seat of her car. She managed to get us all standing in front of the door before it was opened. I was nervous and didn't want to be the first inside but she edged me forward in front of my siblings just as the bolts on the other side were being prized open. My nerves really took a bashing and almost got the better of me. My eyes began to fill with tears, my heart began to pound and suddenly the door was pulled wide open and there standing in front of me was an elderly female, listening as the social worker announced our names and ages. She repeated the name Molly so many times it didn't feel like she had been expecting me, a large part of me hoped they had got it all wrong and would have to return me to Springhill but, of course that didn't happen.

As I looked around, I couldn't help feeling something wasn't quite right. The house inside was far superior to Springhill, luxuriously furnished with the most amazing carved ceilings. The large mantled fireplace housed an open fire that warmed the extended hallway and gave the house a most welcoming feeling, yet, it still didn't feel right.

After saying goodbye to our social worker, we were instantly led away by a round and rather stout lady who had dimples on both sides of her cheeks, she waddled from side to side as she struggled to walk through the hallway and down the corridors. When we reached an enormous room at the back of the house she was wheezing heavily and she gasped for breath as she made an effort to speak. Pausing between each short sentence, she began to explain that the room was our playroom.

As my eyes quickly scanned the room, I saw a long oblong table in the middle, with a row of cupboards either side of it. Beige lino covered the floor and a small children's desk stood alone in the left hand corner. She aggressively pulled up the desk lid and grabbed a handful of children's aprons telling us that we'd be expected to be wearing them before we entered the dining room. She pointed to a door opposite the playroom and informed us it was the toilets, we were expected to keep them clean and weren't allowed to play in there. She ran through so many rules I could barely remember any of them. Then, left us standing in the centre of the room frightened and bewildered. As she walked out of the room she suffered a terrible coughing bout and firmly closed the door behind her.

I was nervous before I had entered the room but even more so once I'd taken stock of everything around me. My eyes wandered around, taking particular note of the large mantled fireplace that stood empty and cold and the two sets of French doors that made the playroom look so inviting from the outside yet, imprisoned me from the inside. Although the room was large and had some furniture in it, there wasn't a single toy in sight. It gave me a kind of cloistered feeling, which felt rather odd considering it was so bright. The house was somewhat unusual with lots of passages and doorways, all leading to the other side of the house. They were cold and uninviting and didn't co-ordinate with the rest of the house. It seemed the further back we got, the less attractive the house became. Doors were locked and keys removed and after living there for a while, I realised it was a house with a difference. It wasn't the locked doors that kept us there against our will but the cruel abuse that was inflicted upon us.

It took us some time to get accustomed to The Outrake Children's Home. There were so many rules it was inevitable that we were going to forget some. The staff were strict and so uncaring, regularly punishing us for things we hadn't achieved and rules we had forgotten but in time I learned to switch off and took each day as it came.

I had only been living there for a short time when I was casually informed I had a 10th birthday drawing near. I had never experienced a birthday before and wasn't quite sure what it entailed, until the day it was upon me then, I was sent to the kitchen to collect my cake. I was excited and felt proud to be treated so importantly. The cake had 10 coloured candles and a smearing of icing sugar, which made it the most beautiful cake I'd ever seen. I picked it up and proudly carried it back to the dining room where Auntie Connie sat at the head of our table. She was the head cook at the home and had baked the cake especially for me. I stood and gazed at it in amazement, taking in every little detail as she slowly lit the candles, one by one. I had never seen anything so beautiful and without hesitation, she announced *"Not only is Molly one year older today, but she also has a beautiful new name, her name is Marie and that's the name she'll be known by."* I couldn't believe what she was saying, it was as if she was determined to upset me and the shameless expression on her face as she glared at me told me she was happy to do what she was doing.

I instantly rejected that name and frowned when I was asked to blow out the candles. I stood in silence as tears trickled down my face, managing to blow out a few of the candles before I broke down and cried. I couldn't understand why she didn't like my name. I'd had it all my life and was anxious to keep it, so I screamed as loud as I could *"My name isn't Marie its Molly, my name's Molly it's always been Molly"*. But Connie raised her voice in anger and repeated her words as the twenty two children anxiously lowered their heads as she callously stripped me of my identity.

As time passed I tried to get used to the name, Marie, but found it difficult to respond to a name I had never heard before; it felt like part of me had died and I had to start all over again. I didn't feel like I knew this little girl, somehow she wasn't the same – little Molly was unique; it was impossible for Marie to be like her. In the past Molly had been so strong and at Springhill she had learned to do things she never thought possible. She had become friendly and fun loving, but Marie wasn't any of those things – she was a stranger, shy and withdrawn and couldn't make friends with anyone. Although I eventually accepted the name, I never knew Marie like I knew Molly.

When I tried to sleep at night I cried but not for Marie. For Molly, the little girl that had lived nine long years through so much brutality and neglect, yet still had the strength to love and care for her younger siblings. Although I tried hard to hang on to her, I felt I had to say goodbye as she slipped back into the past, behind the screen that once protected her. Although I never forgot her, everyone else that ever knew her did. It was easy for them; they were able to wipe away her very existence just by replacing her with a new identity but for me it proved far more difficult.

—◊◊—

CHAPTER 15

Life At the Outrake

I learned like many others had to, that life at The Outrake wasn't easy. Our typical day began when Auntie Jill came thundering up the stairs to wake us at 6.30am. She rattled a large, wooden spoon across the landing radiator before entering each dormitory, screeching, *"Come on you lot, out of bed, rise and shine, hang those nappies on the line"*. I trembled knowing that once she reached my bed she would pull off the blankets, she knew I would have wet the bed and I'd then receive the harshest beating I'd ever had.

The wooden spoon that had become part of her over the years was her instrument for 'light punishment'. However, she carried her favourite leather belt in her apron pocket for when she considered a more severe punishment was appropriate. The large metal catering spoon was kept in abeyance in the back kitchen, especially for those children whom the wooden spoon had stopped having its terrifying effect. At times she gave no reason for beating us, but when she did, it was usually for nothing more than leaving a towel on the bathroom floor, or forgetting to put our toothbrush back into its beaker.

The memory of her has never faded from my mind and I suppose the truth is, it never will. I look back at the things she did and the way she was and I thank my lucky stars, I was born as strong as I was. Other children weren't so lucky; they were a little puny and really screamed out when they were beaten, but my pride suffered more and meant more to me than pain. My ability to endure pain was quite considerable following my early years with Carol, John and my family. I did get quite used to the beatings, although I was always embarrassed at the thought of my pants being removed for the beating. I really did try to stop wetting the bed so that I could go to school without having to hide the welt marks on my skin but over the years I got used to it and submitted to my embarrassment.

Jill was a large robust woman full of anger and so much hate and routinely, she beat every girl on our landing for no apparent reason. Whilst every one of us tried to be first out of bed, dressed and downstairs purposely to get away from her, there was always one unsuspecting youngster, who remained upstairs and suffered the consequences.

I found breakfast times terrifying when she was on duty. I remember sitting at the table, flinching as she marched around the room, slapping the wooden spoon on to the palm of her hand, randomly lashing out at one of us, for not sitting upright or for putting our elbows on the tables. I don't recall her having favourites and as far as I can remember, none of us ever liked her. She was strict and unfair and despite the fact that she beat each of us in turn she seemed to take particular pleasure in beating the younger children, knowing their older siblings would try to protect them and so giving her excuse to beat them too.

It became obvious over the years that at least one of us would be beaten every day before breakfast and we were allowed to leave the room only once she had reduced us to tears. For years the strict rules of The Outrake gave her all the authority she needed to beat the living daylights out of us, for every rule she deemed broken one of us suffered unnecessarily.

I still remember my friend's gross dislike of sausages and couldn't help feeling sorry for her when Jill randomly force fed her with pieces she couldn't stomach. Not surprisingly I find it painful to talk about and no matter how much I try I cannot find words to describe every heartbreaking memory. For years I watched my friends suffer, becoming hardened to their screams and eventually I sensed nothing.

Once my survival instincts kicked in I became cold and callous, showing no concern for any other child apart from my siblings. The Outrake wasn't like Springhill. The staff were hard and bitter, and although they reserved the right to be called 'Auntie' I never felt close to them, like I had with Auntie Gina. I remembered feeling lost and frightened when I first arrived at Springhill, but when I arrived at The Outrake I felt completely deserted. I hadn't been there more than 24 hours before I realised the place had a strange kind of power over all 23 children who lived there. Children moved around the house like controlled zombies and spoke to each other only when staff where out of sight, and even then, it was done quietly beneath their breath. The atmosphere reminded me of my own home when John had been around and although I tried to figure out what kind of a place it was, I was a child and as blind as everyone else, so I couldn't get to the bottom of it.

When I realised there wasn't a single toy in sight tears filled my eyes but somehow I couldn't let them flow, I knew crying wasn't permitted and it was as if everything I had once perceived as being normal was no longer accepted there and a whole new set of life's rules were being hurled at me.

My siblings and I found it difficult to communicate with anyone. Choosing the right things to say and the right time to speak without receiving harsh punishment was a work of art. In my own way I tried to make things easier for my siblings but they were so young they didn't understand and eventually they ceased communicating at all. We couldn't make friends or put our trust in anyone as every single child had to look out for his or herself and had to survive the best way they could, even if it meant informing the staff of others' misdemeanours or trivialities to gain favour. Only on rare occasions did a friendship occur. After years of uncontrolled fighting and malicious name-calling, two children of similar nature would recognise that they were no longer a threat to each other and became bosom pals.

Children do eventually toughen up and we gained support by forming gangs that became part of our everyday lives and the playroom was our battlefield. It was the one place that staff seldom visited, the one place we were often left alone. For years they were oblivious to our conduct; so many young lives were made unbearable, yet not one of us had enough faith in any of the staff to confide in them. Many times I had considered running away but it seemed so far removed from the world I once knew, the fear of getting lost in that wild open countryside helped to keep me locked within its walls.

My own assumptions about the world led me to believe that I wouldn't be there for long. It was that one single thought that gave me the strength to survive the years that followed. Every day I woke up hoping and praying that today was my last day at The Outrake.

As time passed I became more familiar with the children and their stories. Each had a harrowing story to tell and although I had terrible memories of my own, I would listen to their stories with great sadness and regret. Older children tried to show no emotion when remembering their families but I clearly recall the little ones trying hard to keep the last memory of their recently deceased parents alive. These were the unfortunate children that knew The Outrake was all they had and had to accept it for all it was worth. Sometimes I wondered if my life was more difficult than theirs, they had already accepted being alone in the world and had nothing left to hope for. But I still had hopes and dreams that seemed to make my life at The Outrake more unbearable. I still had my parents and dreamt of returning to my family, hoping that one day I might see them again, and although I knew it may never happen I never gave up on that dream. Somehow all the memories of cruelty, neglect and abuse had faded from my mind and had been replaced with all the good and happy times I had experienced at home. The thought of Mother and Father living happily together was at the forefront of my mind, along with the beautiful array of bluebells at Foxen Dam. I remembered our warm and happy Christmases, and the songs Carol sang to help me sleep, all this and more; these were the happy memories I kept inside my head, they were mine and no matter how much I was hurting I knew, no one could take them from me. All the things that had made my life worth living, back then, were once again giving me strength to carry on.

The cruelty of some of The Outrake's staff made my life difficult, but while my head was full of happy thoughts, I remained hopeful for the future. My life was hard, so I found it difficult to remember everything that had happened at home. A lot of my concentration was taken by all the hours I worked in the kitchens and around the house completing chores other children were too young to do, but I used my time in school to regain my strength and rest from the heavy duties which were assigned to me. I learned to do everything I was instructed to do, everything from darning a sock to helping to prepare meals for twenty two children. I found that if I kept busy, time seemed to pass much more quickly. Although I found some things enjoyable, others I found tedious, particularly the times when I felt unwell. Every child who was capable, worked well within their limits, but at times that wasn't enough for the sadistic staff. I was worked so hard, sometimes I felt drained and could have slept on the spot, but staff always remained vigilant to ensure that I didn't.

My chores began early in the morning around 7 a.m. and usually continued until supper at 8 p.m. but the weekends were the most tiring, then I worked most of the day and remained on call even when my own duties where finished. Some days were worse than others, depending on the staff on duty. Jill worked us exceptionally hard, regulating our work and continually finding fault with everything we did and then found pleasure in ordering us to do it all over again before traipsing us half way around the dales in the pouring rain.

Matron usually chose the times for our walks, but sometimes it was used as part of our punishment for when we had made the playroom look untidy or when we didn't pass by her sitting room in total silence, but then a batch of young staff were enrolled and made our walks seem more exciting. Sheila and Elizabeth were locals and knew the dales well, they took it as part of their duty and we visited places we had never seen, occasionally they played games with us, even reciting a little Shakespeare. But I remember that they got the best response from us when they bought us our very first ice cream from the cart at the top of the hill.

After living there for a couple of years I would drift around the house pretending to be an angel, holding my breath as I passed each closed door in silence, I had already stopped communicating and found reticence my only protection. When I first arrived there, I often forgot the golden rule of only speaking when spoken to and when I broke that abysmal silence, a vicious member of staff would charge through a door descending upon me with a rage like thunder. The rage they carried inside them showed heavily on their faces, as they unleashed a formidable fury that not only frightened me, but every child in the house.

While Matron remained in service, staff continually issued punishment without giving us a single kind thought and because of that the house remained forever in silence. We rubbed our limbs where we had been heavily marked and in time we learned to suppress the hurt we felt inside, but as their cruelty got worse we couldn't help releasing some of the tears we had stored behind our bogus smiles.

The long walks that Matron ordered became my lifeline to the outside world and although she couldn't have been aware of it, it was my way of experiencing a little normality, away from the gruelling work and cruelty of her staff. For a while she released us into the open world allowing us to see the children we met in school and speak with hikers who roamed the dales just for fun. The tracks leading to the open caves and white waterfalls that once felt dull and boring to me became one of the most pleasurable experiences of my life. I learned to appreciate nature's beauty and all that it stood for. All the living things that I'd never given much thought to suddenly became part of my world, the vast size and sheer beauty of the open countryside gave me a feeling of excitement, an awareness of freedom that lasted for just a few short hours. The wide flowing river and beautiful valley became a haven for so many of The Outrake children as well as myself. During hours of walking I learned to soak up the beauty and tranquillity of the dales to help me through the difficult times and took advantage of the hours of peace it gave me.

I tried hard to forget that I lived at The Outrake and imagined the countryside soaking up all my fears. Just for a few hours I became someone else, the innocent child I wanted to be. Exploring no man's land, I played with imaginary friends and learned the names of flowers, animals and trees whilst giving lots of thought to other living things that survived among the dales, like I was trying to do. It was taking an interest in the natural beauty surrounding me that helped my time at The Outrake pass more quickly.

I realised once I was away from The Outrake's influence, it had very little power over me and I could be whoever I wanted to be. Although The Outrake had become my home I knew sooner or later, I had to be set free and I could be the person I was born to be.

By the time I was aged twelve I understood that the cruel suffering I was experiencing was a continuation of the abusive experiences I had already suffered as a younger child. It seemed my life wasn't meant to be easy or child-like. Wherever I was, it seemed cruelty and neglect walked hand in hand with me. Regularly singled out I was asked to achieve the most difficult tasks, then, suffered the harsh consequences when I failed.

When the social services rescued me, from the cruelty and neglect of my family, I had been wrong to think I would be safe and that everything would be different. It seemed my life remained the same no matter where I lived. Although I left my family behind that night, the abuse I suffered followed in my shadow, clinging to me like the devil himself.

If it had not been for the short period of time I spent at Springhill I would never have experienced love as it can be and may never have known how it felt to live amongst people who really cared for me. It was Gina who gave me the insight to happiness and helped me realise there was a better life out there somewhere; I just had to find it. I tried to cast dark shadows aside and go in search of the love and kindness I'd been shown at Springhill. But I'd already accepted the fact that human behaviour was so unpredictable, I mistrusted too easily too many people and therefore found it impossible to find what I was looking for.

It seemed my whole life was a test of strength but although I had suffered from cruelty and abuse, I knew I could not afford to give in to it. I had no respect for anyone who mistreated another human being, never mind a child, and often found myself receiving beatings to protect others from what I had suffered for most of my life. Although I was hurt by it, I found the physical pain hurt me far less than the pain I felt inside my heart when I had to stand by and watch my younger siblings being thrashed for something they didn't do. As their screams echoed around the walls of The Outrake, I became less fearful of the evil staff that beat them and as I grew stronger I became more protective of my family.

After two long years I felt myself changing. I was twelve years old and had grown tall enough to gaze into the large hall mirror above the mantle and gazed for some time before I realised the little girl who no longer looked like a child had developed into a fine young lady. My round, chubby face with its rose red cheeks had now been exchanged for a pear shaped smile. My teeth had grown straight and as I took a long hard look at myself, I realised little Molly had long since disappeared and I had become Marie. Beneath my breath I quietly whispered my name, "Molly" but somehow it didn't sound the same. I felt sad for having let her go yet a very small part of me felt happy at the thought of being that much closer to freedom. I was able to count the years I still had to serve, on my fingers – six in all – but it seemed a lifetime away. Although I had never let go of the possibility of returning to my family; something told me it was finally time to let go of any dreams and hopes I had of them rescuing me.

In the three years I had spent away from home I had seen my father only once. Auntie Connie regularly told me he wasn't a well man and found travelling to the dales difficult. On occasions he did write a short letter but his writing was small and difficult to read, but for me the contents of his letters didn't really matter, it was the thought of being remembered that really made a difference. Just knowing that he was still thinking about me made my world a much brighter place. I carried his letters in my school satchel; the only private space I had. They were my prize possessions so I guarded them with my life. I took every opportunity to look at them even though I couldn't read and eventually a girl called Shirley helped me to make sense of them. She had lived at The Outrake for many years and was the closest thing to a friend I had ever known. She helped me to read all that Father had written by spending time teaching me to read comic books her father brought in for her and her siblings at weekends. Although she wouldn't have realised it, she opened up a whole new world for me and within months I found myself reading and writing as well as any other child who lived there. Once I realised I was capable of learning, I became excited and wanted to learn more but I still found difficulty in understanding my peers; as my fear of the seniors seemed to block the whole of my concentration. My communication skills with our elders was very poor, I couldn't even make my teachers understand how desperate I was to progress.

At the end of my first year at Highfields Secondary Modern School for Girls, I awaited the results of my end of year exams. My first result was biology and science which was taught by my favourite teacher, Miss Lawton. I found her classes enjoyable but felt somewhat apprehensive about the results being read out in class. I had always been bottom in all subjects and was ashamed of not being able to do better. As Miss Lawton entered the science lab silence fell amongst us and she addressed our class with politeness and a sense of expertise.

Her voice was clear and although she would normally announce the results in alphabetical order, she took the opportunity that year to announce the results of the girl who had achieved the most progress. I slumped down in my chair feeling totally bored and disinterested as she continued with her acclaim for the girl who was only three marks away from one hundred percent! I gazed into thin air as certain girls' names ran through my mind, bored with the fact that it was usually the same three that achieved higher standards than most; or of course it could have been my friend Shirley – sometimes she did quite well in class. But to everyone's astonishment, including my own, Miss Lawton announced in a very satisfactory manner that it was I who had earned top marks in my first ever exam that year. I was so surprised I almost cried but then I wondered if she had perhaps made a terrible mistake, but after repeating herself and beckoning me over, I stood up with pride and walked towards her to receive my marked papers and her sincere congratulations. She passed me my work and smiled saying, *"I am so proud of you Marie, well done"*. It was at that moment, I realised for the first time in my life I had actually achieved something. Although I was astonished at my results, I sat at my desk proudly hugging my papers as the whole class looked round at me in disbelief. I looked up at Shirley, as for some reason it was important to me that she approved and as my eyes met hers I smiled, knowing it was because of her, that I had fulfilled a small part of my dream. My head was in the clouds that day, so I found it almost impossible to work. I kept on wondering how I had achieved something as important as that, but remained proud of the fact that I had.

I had not expected such high results, although I now realise Miss Lawton had more to do with it than I gave her credit for. She was my form tutor as well as my science teacher, during the first year of attending High School I had always felt comfortable in her presence. Right from the start she instilled confidence in me and even though she was aware of the many problems I had, she never gave up on me.

Within time I felt I owed her something more than just being the typical High school student, so tried my best to learn everything she taught me. Being in the science lab with her was like being on another planet, it was easy to forget what was going on around me when I was engrossed in the experiments we were doing; they never seemed like hard work and I enjoyed them immensely. Miss Lawton was not only an excellent science teacher by whom I feel privileged to have been taught, but she was also the most sincere teacher I had ever met. I remember her showing concern about my low grades in other subjects and randomly asking why that was. For the first time I was being given the chance to talk to someone about my preoccupations and inhibitions and although I wanted to so much, because of my sense of inferiority, I was unable to confide in her; therefore losing the only chance I had of receiving help.

The fear I had of my peers obviously stood in the way of my further progress as I failed terribly in all other subjects, except sport at which I was a natural and in time I became one of the school's top competitors. During my first music lesson I sang solo in front of the whole class. I was petrified at first but after managing to earn myself a permanent place in the school choir, I felt rather proud. I loved singing, it was my life so I felt honoured when I was chosen. Despite being terrified of our music teacher, Miss Lomas, I made every effort to do her proud.

She was very much an old school maid and believed children should be seen and not heard, particularly young girls like us. She was very much part of what we called the gentry and generally looked down her nose at us; even after we had learned to be the young ladies she wanted us to be. Her disappointment with me centred on my maths. Doubling up as my maths tutor she realised my skill at maths was not good hence she repeatedly informed me *"Teaching you Marie is like flogging a dead horse"*. She very often made her concerns known to Miss Lawton, who generally worried about my level of progress and asked me numerous times if there was a reason why I wasn't progressing in any other subject. Although I wanted to talk to her, my long silences displayed my inability to communicate, so she kindly dismissed me. I would walk steadily away from her side knowing I was doing the wrong thing but something inside my head kept telling me no one could really help me. The mourning I felt inside my heart made it difficult for me to speak, so eventually I lost the will and felt a disgrace to everyone who tried to help me.

Attending Highfields School wasn't easy. I recall on my first day the local girls branded me *"one of the Outrake kids"*. There were little things that made us different to the other kids; although we tried hard to fit in it was inevitable that being treated differently would eventually lead to problems. Our identical short-cropped hairstyles and long grey socks with the bright red rings instantly identified us as part of The Outrake clan, so we were not given the respect the other local children received. I found myself retaliating with violence and although I knew it was wrong, it was the only way I knew how to deal with being branded an outcast. Even after a whole year of attending high school I was still isolated by my inability to communicate and it was nearly two years before I made my first friend. Even then she was an outsider like myself and wasn't readily accepted by the other girls.

Our friendship began the day she arrived at our school. Being a city girl she was kind and amusing, not at all shy and had no inhibitions, thus making it easier for me to befriend her. For the short time she attended the school we became inseparable. We had lots in common, including our names, but the teachers didn't think our friendship was good for our development so found it more desirable to separate us in class as our sense of humour frequently disturbed lessons. While she was around I had a strange kind of confidence that I had never before experienced. Other girls referred to us as being rowdies and named us *'the terrible twins' or 'Marie A and Marie B'*. We accepted our appointed nicknames with dignity, having previously made a pact to accept each other as sisters for as long as we lived. Our friendship grew stronger and we developed the kind of personalities that other girls didn't like. While Marie B remained at Highfields I felt confident and reasonably happy. Our friendship lent me the support I needed to forget some of the misery I had been storing inside my head and just for a short while my life actually felt as if it had meaning. Her lively personality kept my spirits high and made me feel quite normal. Although she was aware I didn't live with my own parents, she spoke of the Outrake with great respect and never once made me feel any different to anyone else. She was a caring person who shared everything she had, knowing I had nothing to give her in return. Apart from my devoted friendship, I gave her nothing.

I recall just before her 13th birthday she invited me to her home for tea, but as I had never been outside the Outrake on my own in all the years I had lived there, I knew I would have trouble trying to change the strict ruling that Matron firmly adhered to. I wanted to attend Marie's party but wasn't sure I was brave enough to face the consequence of Matron's brutality if she thought me impertinent for presuming I was someone special. However, with lots of volunteering to do extra chores and regular persuasion from Marie, it took me well over a week to build up the courage to appeal to Matron's better nature. I hoped she would see how important it was for me to receive those few hours of freedom, to spread my wings and feel alive again. After the several days it took her to decide I was overwhelmed when she said I could go. From that day on I could think of nothing but the plans Marie had made for our day. During the last few days before my 'release' I was unable to concentrate on my schoolwork and was regularly pulled aside for my loud, excited giggles as Marie and I planned our day together. I couldn't help wondering what my very first encounter of freedom would feel like after being penned inside those high grey walls of solitude for so long.

On Marie's birthday, I couldn't wait for school to end, I worked extra hard in class to please the teachers and ensured I didn't miss the first bus back to the Outrake. I had my satchel packed and was ready to leave school well before the final school bell rang. I wasn't allowed to sit next to Marie during English so had previously arranged to meet her outside the prefabricated building we used for English. We were both excited and couldn't stop chatting once we had caught the bus. We were anxious to get home but the bus ride from Bakewell to Longstone seemed to take much longer than usual. The old Hully's bus on which we travelled was finding difficulty in getting up the country lanes that evening and I was sure had it not been for the boys of Lady Manners Grammar School chanting their usual amusing Hully's songs, I would never have finished the journey without becoming irritable.

As the bus pulled up, outside the quaint little cottage where Marie and her family lived, I couldn't help thinking what a waste of time it was my going all the way back up to The Outrake, just to have to walk back down again. But Matron had made it abundantly clear I was to return to The Outrake before attending Marie's party, so knowing I'd better not disobey I remained on the bus waving frantically at Marie as she stood and watched the bus draw away from the old memorial, then disappear from view. The old bus took its time struggling up the hill until eventually The Outrake came into view.

Wasting no time I moved to the front and was first off the bus as soon as it came to a standstill. I ran through the side gate to the back of the house and flung open the cloakroom door, peeling off my blazer as I ran. I hung it on the pegs above the long row of wooden seats, on which I flopped in order to remove my shoes. Reaching beneath the seats for the bag of shoe polish, I cleaned my shoes, knowing that Matron would ask if I'd completed my chores before she'd allow me to go. The rest of the children followed me into the cloakroom, one by one, and mournfully moped while I rushed around, I'd never seen them look so sad. The bewildered look written on their faces told me they couldn't understand how I had managed to obtain a few hours away from the house without having to run for it. I knew from the look in their eyes they were envious; but I couldn't blame them for that.

I cautiously walked through the hallway towards the back kitchen hoping to sneak upstairs and change into my play clothes, before Matron could see me. I knew it was never too late for her to change her mind and it wouldn't take long for her to make such a decision, so I tried to get past her and out of the house before she could do that. As I crept through the passage ways, I wasn't surprised to hear the sudden echo of her voice calling my name as I walked towards her office. It seemed she had the power of x-ray vision and was able to see me clearly through the structure of the building. It wasn't unusual for her to correctly identify us as we quickly shunt past her office, trying our best to be elusive. Knowing I was being summoned to her side the fluttering of my heart began well before I reached her office door, I felt physically sick as I nervously knocked seeking permission to enter. For a few seconds I stood fidgeting in front of her before letting out a nervous response to her call and replied *"Yes, Matron?"* in my usual frightened manner. I looked down at her and couldn't help focusing on the extremely large wart she had on her forehead. Her desk was laden with letters and writing paper and I scanned over many documents before smiling to gain her favour. As she looked up, her face remained formal and dignified as she strictly ordered me to wear my Sunday best, reminding me, I only had two hours; including the walk to and from my friend's house.

Showing my appreciation, I thanked her repeatedly before leaving her office. I hadn't much time, so took only a few minutes to run upstairs and change into my lemon dress as ordered, then, back to say goodbye to her and the staff. I couldn't believe the time had come for me to venture through those large gates, I was so excited yet, I trembled with fear. It had been a few years since my social worker had first driven me through them and up the driveway, but the time had come for me to walk back through them on my own.

I walked down the long driveway towards the gates looking back over my shoulder towards the house, wondering if I dare do this. It felt so strange. Although I really wanted to run, my fear of the unknown was stronger than my will to go through those gates alone. Over the years they had deprived me of so much freedom, I hated the very sight of them. The stillness of the countryside was almost frightening, I gasped for breath as I gazed into the wild outdoors. Trying hard to maintain my toughened exterior, I plucked up the courage and ventured over the threshold leaving The Outrake and its grounds behind me, and with the joy of spring and the wind in the air, I floated gracefully into the beautiful heights of freedom.

With the sun on my face and the breeze in my hair, I took flight and ran as fast as I could away from the house that held me prisoner. The distance that grew between the house and myself, wasn't enough until it was well out of sight; even then the dark shadow it cast over my soul remained with me.

It was extraordinary, that first hint of freedom reminded me of the past, way before my life was stolen by people who thought they had the ability to care for me, but who actually didn't. Such a special moment, it seemed the birds had flocked together to sing a chorus especially for me, this was a day I shall always remember.

I cried my first tears of happiness, as I roamed the country lanes like it was my second nature. No doubt I had become a wild child and no amount of taming would ever replace the pleasure I felt, I was free underneath those beautiful blue skies of infinity.

For the first time ever, I was able to observe the tiny cottages dotted around the village. They were unusually small, but pretty too and the colours used to decorate the unused troughs and milk churns only added extra beauty to what was already a near perfect landscape.

Never before had I walked a mile and three quarters in such a short space of time. I arrived at Marie's home in good time and was pleased to find her anxiously waiting outside for me. She looked quite different. I had never seen her outside school, so wasn't accustomed to seeing her in jeans and jumper. She looked even more petite than she did in her uniform and made me feel rather corpulent. Her dark curly hair was something to be admired and suited her well. As I walked towards her I literally felt her loud contagious laugh echoing all around the village, encouraging me to giggle heartily, well before I got near her. The very second I reached her she grabbed my arm, pulling me into her home to meet her family. Her mother was tiny and looked almost identical to Marie, but her older brother was tall and didn't resemble her at all. He was very polite although I felt somewhat uncomfortable in his presence. However, Marie's outrageous personality disguised any embarrassing situations that arose and I soon felt at ease.

Her home was small, and although a little over-crowded with furnishings, it felt so much better than The Outrake, as it had natural warmth that made me feel at home and pleasantly comfortable. It felt good to be among a real family again. Although there was sibling rivalry I had enough intuition to know that the respect they showed to each other was natural.

The meal that Marie's mother cooked for us was very simple yet, I felt peculiar not being asked to assist while the meal was being prepared. I wasn't used to sitting idle while watching someone work, and it felt rather unnatural, considering I had worked in a kitchen most of my life. Somehow her mother sensed my awkwardness, so in order to ease that, she suggested we visit the park until tea was ready. Marie jumped at the chance, but not before she suggested we swapped over our clothing. She was fascinated by the layers of chiffon and lace, from which my yellow dress was made up of and wouldn't take no for an answer. I tried to refuse as I was sure her clothes wouldn't fit me, but Marie was adamant they would.

She looped her arm through mine like she did at school and pulled me into their bathroom helping me to change. We laughed and giggled as we fell over each other in the attempt to exchange clothing in the smallest room I had ever seen. I was surprised when I was able to pull on Marie's jeans although the zip wouldn't meet, the button at the waist ensured they remained fastened. Her jumper was rather large and so fitted me perfectly.

Marie looked beautiful in my dress yellow which suited her so much better than it did me. Within minutes of me fastening it, she was outside showing it off to everyone. She thought it far more beautiful than anything she had ever worn. I was puzzled, wondering what it was that made her feel so special in a dress that I hated so much. I couldn't understand her parading around the village in a dress I felt so ridiculous in.

I sometimes wondered if, over the years of being institutionalised, I had become ungrateful or unappreciative. I remembered when I was at home I had longed for a dress like that but now things were different. I would have swapped the dress a thousand times over, just to live with my family the way she did.

At the park, Marie whirled and whirled around the swings, singing and dancing, looking much happier than I had ever seen her before. Suddenly I realised I had never given much thought to her personal circumstances and although she never spoke much about herself, I suppose I had been too engrossed in my own problems to have considered that it might have been possible that Marie's life wasn't all that I presumed it was. Although she referred to her mother quite often, she had never mentioned her father or his whereabouts. Remembering the short time I was allowed to be away from The Outrake, Marie suggested we went back to her home for tea. Having one last go on the swing, I worked up to a ridiculous height and jumped, clearing a large area of the park before I landed heavily on the grass in front of her. We laughed, looped our arms and strolled across the grass as if we had forever.

I was quite surprised how relaxed I felt considering I had lost a lot of my confidence over the years. I seemed to fit in with her family quite well and although the two hours leave from The Outrake didn't give us much time to talk, we still had lots of fun. Neither of us wanted the day to end but I would have been foolish to think that delaying my return to The Outrake would have been beneficial to me. Having changed back into my own clothes, I thanked Marie's mother for having me and said goodbye to Marie and her brother.

I really hated The Outrake and all kinds of thoughts went through my head as I waved reluctantly to Marie and her family, but as usual I kept my feelings well hidden. I could barely face the thought of going back and as I walked away from them I felt a large lump develop at the back of my throat, and as I desperately tried to hold back my tears I felt the warmth of a single tear trickle down my cheek.

We waved to each other until I had turned the corner and was heading towards Little Longstone, which would have been like paradise had it not been for The Outrake residence. Once they were out of sight I began to cry and quickened my step to ensure I wouldn't be late, as I knew Matron would punish me if I dared to be late. My tears fell as free as rain from the sky as I walked back to The Outrake, wishing with all my heart that I was part of Marie's family instead of my own. It was only when I was alone I was able to cry. The Outrake had made me so unhappy over the years I found it difficult to describe my innermost feelings to anyone and I could never have put my sorrow into words, even if my life had depended on it.

Suddenly, I find my concentration has been broken, unfamiliar warmth fills my heart and I smile, remembering all the years I had tried to come to terms with my life. My mind drifts to the very beginning of my story, when I was too frightened to converse with anyone, but suddenly I feel strong, free of all the pain and misery I have been burdened with most of my life. I sit and listen to the birds whistling outside my window, sounds I haven't heard for many years, feeling really pleased with myself for having the courage to write my memoirs. I suddenly realise I fear nothing, not even my brother

John. Strange! Inside my head I no longer hear little Molly screaming and babies crying, just silence! Perfect silence!

As time moved on and I got older I tried to forget my family, to live my life without regrets, but The Outrake staff made that impossible. They were blinded by their duties, ignorant to our past and cruel in every sense of the word. Every child who had been condemned to that place, grieved deeply for their families and spent years full of anguish and regret, and had it not been for the varied few special people, I'm sure we children would not have survived.

I arrived back on time that night, but no one seemed to notice; it was as if I hadn't even been away. I automatically joined the other children in the playroom, knowing it was near bedtime. Jumping up onto the lockers, I sat gazing through the French windows onto Mr Tim's farmland, wondering how long it would be before I was able to taste that freedom again. I felt a strong sense of loneliness as I thought about Marie with her family and wondered what life would be like for me outside those walls.

I yearned to be set free, to live a normal life among normal people. As the overwhelming feeling of sadness returned, I swallowed hard in an attempt to disguise my sudden urge to break down and cry. My desire to leave The Outrake had become an obsession. My mind constantly thought of ways to break free, yet I had known for some time that my family home no longer existed, so even if I had managed to get away, I would have had nowhere to go. I was trapped within the authoritarian system and there was nothing I could do about it.

The Outrake staff spent years moulding me into an entirely different person to whom I was deep inside. I was no longer the audacious child I used to be, but a child whose mind had been twisted to form identical characteristics to many other children who had been resident there for years. Having always been a child with a difference, I fought long and hard to keep my individuality although there were times when I became so confused, I really didn't know who I was. I wasn't sure whether the lifestyle there was normal, as having been abused and neglected for the largest part of my young life, I had very little to compare it with. Up to the age of twelve I had seen so many children damaged by severe brutality I expected nothing better.

Of the twenty three children resident at The Outrake I was the child that seemed most disparate although I tried to fit in. My strong personality fought against the expectations everyone had of me. I tried to play with dolls and enjoy childlike activities but I really didn't feel comfortable doing either. I had always been mature for my age and found it more natural to be a carer rather than be cared for. Although I was only twelve I felt strange being among older children who still played 'Ring a ring a Roses' and 'Oranges and Lemons'. At times Matron encouraged group activities, but only when the local authorities came to inspect the home. Welfare visiting times seemed very important; it was when Matron showed us lots of attention and taught us how to play games we would normally be punished for. I felt embarrassed playing games I believed were for younger children, therefore spent time knitting alongside Shirley and occasionally practising on the old piano, a new addition to the playroom.

Once Matron had finished her guided tour and the welfare inspectors had left, she called for silence and instructed the staff to maintain their usual strict authority over us. She was more than satisfied that they were capable of running the home without her, as she had taught them well. She was confident their harsh and cruel activities controlled us to the extent that we dare not speak or shed a tear, so they needed very little intervention from her.

We saw very little of Matron outside the comfort of her own sitting room. Her presence in the playroom was unusual, it caused a lot of tension and disturbed us considerably so we recognised it as being significant. Many of us suffered from nervousness, but we learned to hide it well, as any signs of sickness or unnatural weakness was treated with further harsh discipline from the staff. Failure to respond to such discipline was generally seen as a counter-action against them and although many of us were weak we would transmit courage from one to another giving each other the strength to survive the brutality we suffered.

In retrospect I now realise how much we needed each other; the fights and aggression we displayed were used only to protect ourselves. Emotionally we had been destroyed and although it didn't seem much like it at the time, just being there, sharing each other's pain, divided the hurt between so many, thus lessening the full impact of the staff's brutality; making our lives bearable.

—⁓—

CHAPTER 16

Memories

When I first arrived at the Outrake I had been expected to fit in and become just like everyone else but I never settled and my heart was always set on leaving. I had no conception of time and was unaware how long it took to convince everyone I really didn't belong there. I cherished some memories of my family and spent hours every day thinking about Simon whom I hadn't seen for over four years, since our separation at Springhill. Despite the years we had spent apart I constantly wondered about him. I remembered every detail of his tiny face; he was never far from my thoughts and my tears flowed freely at the slightest memory of him. I felt sure I would see him again but as the years passed I came to realise that the Simon I knew was lost to me forever. I wept in remembrance of the baby brother I was lucky enough to have had and loved for just a short time and thanked God for giving him to me.

The days were long and the years seemed many, I was glad at times for the extra chores I was given as they helped to fill my days and it was far better than sitting in the playroom gazing through the windows. I spent a lot of my time sitting in that playroom, as there was no encouragement to do anything else. Day after day, week after week, I gazed across farmland looking through the bold and strong branches of the huge oak tree that stood proud in Mr Tim's field, and I came to think of that oak tree as an old friend who was always there for me. Miles of countryside separated me from civilization; but I could not have chosen anything more beautiful to stand in my way. I knew that land better than most and as the seasons rapidly changed, I watched the land bed down each winter. Inside the house time stood still, and had it not been for annual events that took place around the village during the years I would have found it impossible to believe my life still went on.

I was almost a teenager and attending senior school so the changing of the seasons was rarely mentioned and time didn't have any great significance. I knew it rained in April and snowed in December but it wasn't paramount to know. In time I lost all recognition of the seasons, no longer knowing in which month they came and although I felt happier when it snowed at Christmas, I felt sad when I no longer remembered which month the sun would shine.

I remembered the summer holidays and occasional picnics that always had their downsides and wept as I recalled my first visit to the sea. I remember thinking that Bacton was a strange choice of place to take so many children, it was quiet and nothing much to do there. Lotty, a new member of staff, put pay to any plans we had made and ruined what should have been one of the happiest times of my life. I'll never forget my little sister's screams echoing around the camp site as blood poured from her mouth. She stood in front of me paralysed with fear, unusually pale and darkened eyes, begging me to rescue her as Lotty forced a large proportion of urinated sheets into her mouth knocking several of her teeth to the ground. Screaming and shouting she forbade Lorraine to wet the bed ever again. Overwhelmed with pity I stood vacant for a while, trying to take in one of the most inhumane acts of cruelty I had ever witnessed up to that time. Then I broke down and cried, not just for my sister but for myself too.

At times I would feel the coldness of the linoleum on the back of my legs as I sat hunched against the playroom window. Clearing the heavy condensation away from the window I viewed Mr Tim in his field that was heavily bogged down by the heavy fall of rain we'd had that year and he looked cold and lonely. I gave a kind thought to the new lambs that had recently entered the world and watched their mothers as they found them shelter under the large oak tree. The bouncing rain upon the windows produced enough sound to cover my gentle whimpering as tears trickled down my face as the pity I felt for the lambs overwhelmed me. The land would suddenly be adorned with a blanket of bulbs as their vibrant colours made me aware that once again spring was upon us. For me Mr Tim's lambs were always the first telltale sign of spring and the start of another year. It was often the time when I felt most lonely as the heavy rains seemed to cloud my thoughts. As I gazed into the clouded skies, I wished my time at The Outrake to pass more quickly. With my eyes wide open and my heart firmly closed I allowed my memories of spring in Foxen Dam woods to drift in and out of my mind like a dream untold, yet I could not allow those memories to fill my heart with sadness, as they were the happy places I held dear to my heart and would always remember them as my treasured havens.

My world of private thoughts helped me to survive a life I could not have otherwise beaten, I was proud and strong, but without my memories I'm sure I would not have survived.

My relationship with some of the staff improved over the years, they got to know me well and realised that I no longer feared them as I had done in the past. Although their authority still remained over the majority of the children, their power over me was limited, yet I still weakened as I witnessed them strike younger children who were helpless and unprotected. It seemed to be that once we had reached a certain age we became exempt from the physical violence they previously used to terrorise us. As I approached my teenage years I realized any dreams I had for my future got further and further away. I had been caged like an animal and given no free-dom to learn any abilities and skills that I might have had, had I been able to choose my own path. One thing of which I was sure, I could never enter the cruel world of caring for damaged children; if it meant I had to be barbaric. Each morning I awoke and felt cursed with the feeling of hopelessness as I witnessed the suffering of so many innocent children. Their pain seemed everlasting, not only from yesterday's beatings but also from that morning's procedure. I would cringe as I walked past the boys' bathroom, knowing my younger brother Andrew would once again be sitting in the bath tub, raw with cold, following the hours he sat among buckets of ice and frozen water. I watched how Jill and many of the other staff cruelly dragged his weak and frozen body over the side of the bath, just to beat him one more time for nothing more than uncontrollable incontinence. As I prepared myself for school, I wept as images of Andrew covered in red, blue and purple bruising constantly flashed through my mind. I realised they were the results of prolonged exposure to severe cold, so I cursed the staff for being undeniably cruel.

Although I no longer feared the staff, I knew any interference from me would certainly result in further retribution for Andrew. I had lost count of the times I had told him to be more like me, to hide his fear and fight back, hoping it would give him the same protection that I had, but it was difficult remembering what it had been like for me at his age. I had forgotten how many times I had been beaten for wetting my bed and could only hope he would eventually develop enough strength to protect himself, just as I did. Until then he slotted into the category of children who were regularly beaten for what I considered to be normal behaviour for their ages.

I hated the staff much more for beating my siblings than I ever did for beating me. If I had been five years older I could have taken my siblings and saved them from this torment worse than hell, but I wasn't all grown up and although I felt responsible, I was just a little girl who had nowhere else to go. I couldn't begin to understand how they felt when I stood and watched them tolerate the staff's chosen punishment, when they had done so little wrong. Just being children, they could not have expressed in words any more clearly than the grave expressions they had on their faces as they suffered blows to their bodies, aimlessly trying to protect themselves. The hate I felt for each member of staff enabled me to hide any sign of weakness in their presence but as they deliberately scarred each child for life, I felt the fury within me become venomous. I had no way of hiding the truth. I was just one of those kids whose facial expressions had a habit of letting them down. Even when I tried to pretend I was impartial to their bullying, it was plain for them to see that I hated them for it.

After years of putting up with their ability to cause pain and suffering to so many of us I decided to make a firm promise to myself that I would never allow any member of staff to hurt me again, even if it meant retaliating. I always remembered a quotation my mother repeated over and over again when I was so young and still lived at home, 'An eye for an eye, a tooth for a tooth', and although I knew this would warrant further punishment, I still made it clear to them that I had limitations and would no longer tolerate their inhumanity.

Over the years, it seemed I had spent most of my time mistrusting the whole world and now I was well into my teens, I longed for people I could confide in. The thought of meeting a sweetheart had crossed my mind but apart from the gardener and our cleaners, I had no contact with anyone. I knew the teachers' policy was to inform Matron of any problems that arose in school, so I was reluctant to talk to them as the repercussion of involving outsiders could have been far worse than the problem itself. So I turned my attention to a young man who visited The Outrake at weekends. Although he was a little older than I, he seemed smitten by me and watched as I went about my chores. I'd been isolated for years and so found it difficult to approach him and I was unable to speak up for fear of being rejected. It took me months of writing silly little messages on scraps of paper, rolling them up into tiny balls and throwing them in his direction before I learned that he was Colin Willis from Litton. Although he was respectable and willing to communicate with me, I was extremely shy and found it impossible to speak with him. It was at this stage of my life, I first realised my own inferiority played a huge part in my inability to communicate, resulting in frustration that gave way to long bouts of sadness and aggressiveness that I found difficult to control. As I matured, the more problematic I became and yet no one but I could accept that my development was somewhat unnatural in comparison to other normal, outgoing teenage girls.

The staff still treated me like a child but I no longer thought of myself as such, my previously chubby frame had now developed into an hourglass figure and I had already begun my menstrual cycle. I had been masturbating from a very early age and although I found an element of comfort in what I was doing, I could not eliminate the excitement I felt as I fantasised my way through an orgasm. I made regular times for my pleasuring, usually when other children were asleep, but sometimes it proved difficult and they made it obvious they were aware of my actions. Although many of them where much older than I, they hadn't yet reached the same level of maturity and enjoyed making fun of me, causing me to feel ridiculous and, at times, abnormal. I was the youngest girl in the dormitory but it seemed my sexual development was far above average and had been since I was sexually abused as a young child.

I was almost thirteen before staff noticed physical changes in me. The little smocks I was forced to wear no longer concealed my growth and although Shirley, Susan and I were basically the same age, I looked much older than them. Matron had a clever way of restraining our maturity and scornfully objected when we made attempts to look our age. I began to feel silly wearing the frilly dresses she chose for us to wear at weekends, they where childish and looked rather old fashioned so, at that stage, I was only too pleased to be isolated. I felt ashamed of the way I looked, it seemed I had grown up before my time and the dresses they chose were designed to cover my development, so I felt embarrassed to have people around me and began to withdraw from activities that showed my bodily developments and maturing proportions.

But I recall one evening when we returned from school, I was told to enter "Miss Ashford-in-the-Water" competition, when for the first time I was allowed to wear an outfit suitable for my own age, a purple A-line skirt and a checked blouse that had been bought specifically for me. On the night of the competition I felt reasonably confident and looked really grown up but only managed to take second place in the competition. I wasn't disappointed as the children I went to school with really made my night. For the first time ever they accepted me for who I was and treated me as their friend. Instead of just 'one of the outcast kids' I suddenly became the one they were all cheering for. It was during that evening I noticed my clothing played a significant part in being accepted. I had never given it much thought before, but learned that the old - fashioned clothing we usually wore left us wide open to ridicule. The village folk had no idea the clothing wasn't ours and they associated it with a much lower status than their own. Compared to their standards, I must admit we looked very archaic and I really couldn't blame them for sniggering.

After that night I gave a lot of thought to my appearance and began to think of a way of becoming the person I wanted to be, closely observing everyone I came into contact with. I chose their most striking features, and stored them inside my head so that when I needed to I could return to them to choose an identity of my own that would please everyone. I had spent so many years around people I didn't like I had already decided the kind of person I didn't want to be and was fully determined not to be like anyone I knew, but I was influenced by the secretarial types who travelled alongside me on the school bus. I stored as much of their charm as I could inside my head and went to work on producing the person I thought I should be. After all, how was I supposed to grow up normal, once I'd been stripped of all my best attributes?

The only thing I had never been stripped of was my voice. When I sang I felt proud knowing it was the most natural thing about me, and I was pleased I had managed to hang on to it for so long. Singing had always been part of my world and I knew if there really was a God then it must have been him who gave me such a gift. I was praised for my singing and overwhelmed when Mrs Arnfield first asked me to sing 'Amazing Grace' during the Harvest Festival. I rehearsed until I was sure I had it right and on that Sunday I was proud to represent the Outrake kids in chapel. I sang from the heart, knowing it was my only chance to prove to the local people that we children who lived beyond that old grey wall were as much part of God's work as they themselves were.

That Sunday proved to be a blessing in disguise and although our little chapel rarely attracted people, it over-flowed with newcomers. The posters that Mrs Arnfield had placed around the village attracted so many, that the chapel could barely house them. With my help Mrs Arnfield was able to open the doors of our little chapel for a few more years, without the loss of its congregation.

The Harvest Festival was the one thing we Outrake children looked forward to and because of its popularity it helped us all to overcome the embarrassing stigma that went with being a *'child in care'*. In 1971, for the first time I sang solo at our Harvest Festival, and following its great success a child sang each year thereafter, building up a reputation for the young singers of The Outrake Children's Home.

I often wondered why Mrs Arnfield chose me that year. I wasn't the easiest child to teach; I was shy and a little stubborn, and although I sang well I was sure I had no other qualities. Still, she saw in me something that gave her the hope she needed to keep our little chapel alive. I had never done anything like that before but it felt good being singled out and knowing she had enough confidence in me to pull it off. During my practice sessions I got to know her and became rather attached to her, she was kind and gentle and her caring, thoughtful ways won my full co-operation.

A few weeks later she presented me with a gift, a silver necklace that she placed into my hands and quietly said, *"Marie, you should smile a little more often, those sad eyes do not coincide with such a beautiful voice. Thank you, your mother would have been proud"*. The word 'mother' gained my full attention and my curiosity began to unfold. I quizzed her about any knowledge she had of my mother and my home town and it wasn't long before I realised her sudden appearance at the chapel wasn't the first time she had seen me. Being a district nurse and nursing officer she had spent many years working in and around the community in north Derbyshire, visiting my mother following the birth of my siblings and I. At first I felt a little giddy at the thought of being recognised, but a larger part of me felt embarrassed as I suddenly realised she must have been aware of my abused upbringing. Although she treated me with respect I felt humiliated, knowing she held so much knowledge of me. But she had a way with children that could only be admired, her softly spoken voice gave me comfort and within minutes I had forgiven her for the knowledge she unfortunately held. I had always liked her but admired her even more for absorbing the history of my family and accepting it with such equanimity, she showed no sign of pity or disgust and for that she deserved all the respect I knew how to give.

After all the years I had spent surviving the life of an abused child, I realised the end was near. It was Matron who had held this terrifying fort together and although she tried hard to hide her unsteady hand, she was old. I felt no shame for the thoughts I had of her and in a most peculiar way, my hate had somehow turned to pity. I knew she found it difficult to come to terms with her retirement so a very small part of me felt sad that she had to. I knew I would never forget her and I tried to forgive all her cruel ways, but all the bitter memories that had poisoned my mind against her remained fixed within my thoughts.

Although I could never have loved her, I feel sure that my mind could have filtered the good from the bad, if only she had shown a little compassion. My heart was filled with so much bitterness I found it hard to care about what might become of her. Although her hands rarely lifted the instruments of punishment, her unquestioned decision to have us flogged remains a terrifying memory lodged deep within my mind. Still my tears roll freely down my cheeks as my memories become clouded with a deep sadness of what might have been. I had wished so many times for a life without her, not realising how much her life had already influenced mine. The things she had taught me stood me in good stead; I knew how to make jam from the picking of the fruit to the labelling of the jars and could whip fresh milk into cream better than anyone and although my manners slipped once in a while, I managed to adjust well to her reserved way of thinking. However, her cruelty still taunts my brain, even though a small part of me needs to forgive her.

Many weeks passed before Uncle Dave arrived. I believed him to be Matron's replacement, though only temporary and he held no control over us whatsoever. He had replaced every closed door with a large wooden wedge, which enabled us to flit swiftly from one room to another without feeling intrusive and gave us the go-ahead to run and have fun; something he knew we had done very little of. He arrived with lots of new ideas, most of them as crazy as he was. In all the years I had lived at The Outrake, I had never seen anyone chase all twenty three children around the house like he did. Hide and seek became a firm favourite and lasted for hours every day. Of course, he was the nominated seeker and never complained as he bubbled with laughter, searching the house for each and every one of us.

Within a matter of weeks he undid everything Matron had worked so hard to achieve, but in doing so, he gave us our first taste of freedom, he pinned back the large blue gates that had kept us locked within those walls for too many years. It took so little time for us to take advantage of his kindness and after a few weeks we had become wayward and a little disobedient. We fought hard to gain his individual attention and rebelled if we didn't get it. He was nothing like Matron, he was unreserved, open hearted and believed in goodwill and because of that we loved him and he became our friend.

Unfortunately, our futures didn't lie in the hands of Uncle Dave. After just a few months, the sudden change we had been expecting happened, and although we cried we knew our tears had never changed anything and he left anyway.

It was a few hours later when I realised I was going to miss him more than I thought. Everything was put back to how it was and we slowly returned to our usual morbid state. His absence had brought the house to a standstill and once again I experienced that suffocating silence I had suffered from, so many times before. The loneliness that had become a permanent part of me sunk deeper into the very walls of my heart, paralysing the whole of my senses.

No longer caring what the future had in store for me, I hid myself away behind the large drapes of the dormitory windows, gradually giving way to floods of tears I cried hoping some day he would return. A large part of me regretted caring for him the way I did, it was more likely I would never see him again and I felt sad that I had allowed myself to trust him, when I knew he would eventually walk out of my life just as easily as he had walked into it.

Although it was considered normal for me not to make a friend of him, secretly I had hoped he would make one of me, but he left The Outrake without even considering me. I cried for weeks knowing that this placement meant nothing more to him than just a job. Although part of me couldn't help loving him, I hated myself for it and wished a thousand times I had never set eyes on him. I hated feeling the way I did and although I thought about him every day I knew my hopes of ever seeing him again would never materialise. The usual taint of sadness that I felt prior to his arrival hung around me like a suffocating fog, giving me no incentive to look forward or purpose for living.

Change at The Outrake was inevitable, as one person left, another took their place and Uncle Dave was no exception. In the following weeks, Janet and John Hawkins were assigned to the job and moved in with their seventeen-year-old son Martin. Derbyshire County Council gave no consideration to our thoughts, feelings or ability to cope with the constant changes and our lives where upturned once more to accommodate a family of carers.

I suppose in a way I was lucky, I was almost fourteen and one of the oldest children of the house. I had only a few more years before independence and I couldn't wait! I was so sure that when I was old enough to go it alone, my life would definitely change for the better. I had dreams of what I was going to do and thought how perfect my life would be. My mind played an important part in creating illusions of freedom and happiness, allowing images and thoughts of a perfect, happy home to flood my brain, allowing no room for struggle or disappointments.

But I couldn't see the obvious - how institutionalised I had become! I had no suspicions of the terrible conse-quences it would have on my life thereafter.

―◊―

CHAPTER 17

The Child from My Past

My first impressions of Janet and John Hawkins was a favourable one. They where a middle - aged couple, attractive with perfectly groomed hair and far more lively than Matron ever was, so I thought my life at The Outrake would change for the better. They made it clear to other staff that they disapproved of the archaic style of the house and the way we were being cared for and even informed Mr Hutton at The Derbyshire County Council offices that they didn't feel comfortable with the surroundings. They versed their opinions openly, explaining to him, it was not what they expected and it certainly wasn't in our best interest to be surrounded by such 'doom and gloom'. Most of everything was just as Matron had left it, clean and orderly but Victorian furniture wasn't fashionable at that time and the dark floral furnishings weren't to Janet's taste, so the house was refurbished and looked more welcoming than it ever had.

I saw Janet cry more than once and I thought the sadness in her eyes was because she pitied us, but I was wrong. Although her tears ran freely, her grief was more for her son than for us. She knew he wouldn't be happy living amongst children like us, we displayed so much heartache and sorrow and were far from pleasurable to be around but nevertheless she stayed, modernised the house and tried to make it his home.

I wondered why she wanted to live amongst children like us. I wasn't the brightest of kids, so I had this strange notion that if she hadn't stayed, we might all have been sent home and we'd have lived happily ever after; but that wasn't reality.

Up to that time Matron had been the strongest figure in my life and it didn't take me long to realise that Janet wasn't anything like her. I constantly looked for similarities between the two of them but there weren't any. Although I was always frightened of Matron, I remained grateful for the fact that in all the years I remained at The Outrake she kept me safe from my brother John, but Janet didn't seem strong enough to protect me from anyone and I clearly disregarded her husband, solely because he held the same name as my brother. It took months for them to settle in; although their presence created a few problems most of the children eventually accepted them but I found it more difficult. Their son, Martin, was much older than us and very spoiled, I tried to like him but I just couldn't get on with him. He had this way of making me feel inferior to him and knew exactly how to make me cry; he regularly ridiculed me for living without my parents and just as I began to think my life couldn't get any worse we began to fight. I wasn't pleased that he had formed a close bond with Shirley, she was my only friend and I had this terrible fear of losing her. I hadn't experienced such a strong sense of jealousy before but all of a sudden my emotions seemed to spiral out of control and I began to make trouble for the two of them. We had previously been made aware that none of us were allowed to form close relationships with the opposite sex. I knew that at the age of fourteen Shirley was far too young to be involved with Martin, so at every opportunity I made a sarcastic remark in front his mother and father knowing they would eventually realise that when he and Shirley disappeared into his bedroom, it wasn't just to revise their school work.

I felt sad when he took Shirley away from me. I was lonely and had no one to talk to. At times I'd disappear to the bottom lawn where I rekindled a few of the happy memories I'd had at The Outrake. Feeling very sorry for myself I cried but there was no one ever there to offer me sympathy. I knew by that time, my life at The Outrake would never get any better so I did all I could to get away from there. My presence seemed to irritate Janet and John and I found it hard to communicate with them. I wasn't sure I liked the adjustments they had made and felt my personality had been reformed to the extent where there wasn't room for further change. It was apparent that every individual who became responsible for me had different ideas on how I should behave, so I found it difficult trying to keep up with their expectations. My mind could no longer cope with their demands and I began to feel bitter at the thought of constantly changing everything that felt natural to me; just so I could please others. The older I got, the more difficult it became, until eventually I felt so bad about myself, I stopped caring.

During the last few months I remained at The Outrake, I entered a phase of despondency. It was a feeling similar to that I had when Mother abandoned me some years before. Although I tried to understand why my mind was so unsettled, I could not unravel the distorted and confused thoughts that lurked inside my head. I no longer sat in the playroom gazing through the window across the wild open fields, at a world I felt wasn't ready for me and it was difficult to believe how everything that was once so important to me, now meant nothing. The tiny chapel that often gave me refuge and the bottom lawn that once played a huge part in my life were now things of the past, yet they still fuelled my thoughts with memories I had of them. The long walks through the cornfields and around the dales that once provided me with the knowledge of the beautiful life that existed around them, was now exchanged for Friday night discos and football on the park.

It seemed we had little time to spare for one another and quarrelled repetitively with younger staff. The changes we all experienced were made solely with younger children in mind, giving little thought to myself or any other teenager that remained. My new way of life proved to be something I couldn't get used to, although the freedom to do as I liked felt good for a while. It wasn't long before I faced the most heart-rending change of my life, which made all the freedom in the world feel meaningless.

I had been aware of my own difference for some time. Unlike the other children, I could not relate to Martin or his parents. As young as I was I was already set in my ways, so unable to change into the kind of person they wanted me to be. For years I had been skilfully manipulated by Matron and her staff and had been used to strict guidelines, it was unfortunate I was past the age of change and was left with formal characteristics that no one seemed to like. No matter how much Janet and John tried to twist me, I could not change the person I had finally become. I knew they couldn't understand why I was like I was and I didn't know how to begin to tell them. I only wished I could have given them a glimpse of little Molly. She had been locked up inside me for all those years but in all that time no one had the kindness to release her. I knew if they had known her, they would have liked her, but once I had become Marie, I couldn't change that nor could I blame them for considering me unsuitable to live along side them. I was pleased to be consulted about their plans to have me removed from The Outrake and took pride in making the final decision to go back to Springhill. I'd been happy there and thought I would be again.

Before I left, I was very closely monitored and thoroughly reprimanded for what I perceived to be normal teenage behaviour. I was scared of John and because I'd stop trying, he picked up my every fault and constantly hauled me over the coals for what he considered to be unruly behaviour. I had lived at The Outrake for over four years and was pleased when the gates were finally opened for me. I wasn't sure I was doing the right thing, but a large part of me wanted to be free of its clutches. I was told before I left that someone would be arriving to take my place. Showing little interest, I informed Shirley who had chosen to leave alongside me (she was no longer allowed to see Martin so felt it was the right time to move on). She had lived at The Outrake for eight years and felt the same way about it as I did. We had become quite independent and enjoyed the feeling of being set free, even more so, when we found out we were leaving together. We were roughly the same age and had experienced a lot of the same problems, so decided to choose the same destiny. We no longer fitted in, so when we were given the same choices we took the bull by its horns and chose to move on. We were really excited at the thought of being released and couldn't wait to let everyone know.

The day we left, I couldn't wait to leave school. I said my goodbyes to children I had known for many years and made a firm promise to my younger siblings to stay in touch. I told them I would visit from time to time and they knew I wouldn't let them down, so seemed happy to let me go.

Our transport was due at about 6pm but Janet came to inform us that it would be arriving late. I remember her being rather cross and taking every opportunity to try and upset us before we left. She said she was disappointed in us and assured us that our transfer was best for everyone. She made it clear that neither Martin nor John wanted to say goodbye and would never be seeing us again so it was obvious to me at that stage that my dislike of them was a mutual feeling. I never got on with Martin and I had always felt uncomfortable in John's presence so that meant nothing to me. I only ever saw John when I had to, perhaps when he chose to assist Janet in telling me off or when he felt the need to reprimand me for my sarcastic comments, so I was glad to be leaving without further embarrassment of seeing him again, but Shirley seemed a little hurt by it.

I think it was the nonchalant look on my face that made Janet angry as she spurted out her next sentence, but I heard very little, apart from, "your brother Simon". Then I wondered if I was making one hell of a mistake. I hadn't seen Simon since he was a baby and suddenly, over four years later, he was one of the new children who was coming to live at The Outrake in my place. I fell silent for a while, forgetting how unhappy I'd been. I wanted to ask if I could stay, but I couldn't find the words. Again my pride got in the way and I found it impossible to lower the barrier that had been protecting me for all those years. I stood and stared at her as she spun words like spinning wool and I began to cry, taking in all she was saying, tears streaming down my face on to the playroom floor, knowing by this time that her heart was cold and she wasn't a bit concerned about the hurt she caused me. In the short time she had been at The Outrake I had managed to remain strong but at that very last moment her insensitive words broke my heart. I turned away from her trying to remember how many years I had not seen him, wondering what he might look like, and I broke down sobbing. I had now proved to her that I was human after all. I managed to shrug away from her as she tried to console me, feeling certain her attempt to sympathise was only an afterthought, I found it impossible to allow her to embrace me.

At that moment I hated her so much I am sure I could have killed her. The only consolation I had was that I would see him before I left and he would finally be reunited with Andrew and Lorraine. Walking carelessly towards the playroom windows I gazed through my flood of tears towards my old oak tree, wondering if it would help me remember how many times I had looked through that same window, wishing for that day to come. I wasn't sure who I felt most sorry for, Simon or myself, all I knew was whoever was responsible for mapping out our lives certainly knew how to deal the most cruel and unexpected blows. This was the worst thing that could have happened. Although I had dreamed so often of seeing him again, I was sure that when I did I would never have to leave him.

He was six years old, so I guessed he wouldn't remember me although I hoped he would. I knew it was possible that I wouldn't recognise him but after staring through the window for a full hour, I gave up on him. I was used to disappointments so wasn't surprised he hadn't arrived by 7pm. Arrangements very often didn't turn out the way they were planned, so I knew there was a probable chance he wouldn't arrive at all. Trying hard to hide my disappointment, I walked through to the empty cloakrooms to remove my blazer when Shirley approached me with a smile and considerately announced that my brother had finally arrived.

I was frightened but excited and quizzed her anxiously about his looks. I couldn't wait to see him, but she described him perfectly. My tiny brother had beautiful, olive coloured skin, and handsome looks, his bloodshot eyes were red and swollen from the hours of crying but he was so lovely. How could I have thought it possible I might have forgotten him, when he had been such an important part of my life? Simon regained my affection instantly, the maternal instinct I had all those years ago returned as if he had never been away, but it was when he called me mummy that I knew he hadn't forgotten me, although I had to correct him when the other children laughed. I felt glad that even after five long years he had some recollection of me but there was still a strange feeling of sadness between us. As we both stood, subdued in each other's arms I gently swayed from side to side as I'd done all those years ago, remembering how much it had soothed him. I tried to explain to him that I was his sister but it was clear to me that he had no perception of the word. He told me of the faceless shadows and the lady with the dark brown hair who had haunted him most of his life. Hoping I could give face to his ghosts he uncovered many memories of our haunted past which played havoc with our minds. I was just 14 years old, nursing the child from my past, knowing he would always be a special part of me I found it almost impossible to allow them to separate us again, but I was still a child myself, locked within the care system. My conscience still battled with right and wrong, life had been unfair I knew that, but now, surely it was time to put things right. I had wondered many times who held the key to our happiness, the key that operated so many doors for children just like us. As I sat and nursed my family's youngest member, I felt sure that one day that same key would open the door of kindness for us too. It was at that moment I realised I was destined to leave The Outrake on that day, if only to allow my little brother's life to move forward. Up until then, he had experienced so many disruptions to his life he hadn't felt part of anyone's world, so The Outrake gave him the family he yearned for. Yet from me, in that moment it took so many things, including my future.

When I finally said goodbye to The Outrake, I didn't realise how much of it I was taking with me, the awe of the place had been driven so deep, I carried the scars of troubled emotions, my feelings of fear and morbid admiration was part of my life forever.

I arrived at Springhill late that same night, only to find, that after five long years it had changed more than I'd expected. A few of the same staff remained but I found it difficult to get on with them. It wasn't anything like I had remembered, apart from the children coming and going as quickly as they had always done, nothing remained the same. I found I was no longer one of the youngest and because I had reached puberty the rules were totally different. The staff tended to watch over me with caution, being a teenage girl I was expected to be rough and rowdy but above all, procreative.

Even though I still found it difficult to communicate or confide in anyone, I found my feelings had remained the same for Auntie Gina. She was still the kind and considerate person I had got to know during my previous stay and she gave me the same respect that she had always given me.

I remembered that Springhill had once given me the stability I needed and I thought it would again, but at that moment in time it was so different. My stay was made difficult, trying to match up to older girls who expected me to fight to protect myself, but I was no match for them. My friend Shirley didn't even make it through the night. She had been totally unprepared for the girls' sudden burst of violence and couldn't tolerate their constant provocation. The instigators were older and much bigger than we were, so even though I tried fighting back I couldn't do it on my own. The following morning Shirley was reallocated for her own safety and because I felt threatened being left alone I agreed to fight each girl one by one, just to try and gain dominance over them. This was the way it worked in places like that – it was very much a case of hurt, or be hurt. Although I made a stand at the home, there were two seventeen-year-olds I couldn't master so I did the sensible thing and agreed to be their lackey until the day they left.

I remembered life at Springhill had been wonderful for me when I was aged nine, but at fourteen, it seemed a long way from home. I had reached the age where children like me fought for recognition and staff no longer realised how difficult it was to be "a child in care". Despite their low opinion of some of us, we had hearts of gold and if only they had reached out, they would have found children to love under those hard exteriors. I must admit I found it difficult showing love and affection when pain and suffering was all I knew. But as a child born into so much hate and abuse, I gave only what I knew and expected nothing more. It was only my determination that helped raise me from the gutter whence I had been born, so I knew that when I left Springhill I had to be strong if I wanted to survive the forthcoming changes.

I had my whole life ahead of me. I was finally free of The Outrake and planned to make my life as happy as I had always dreamt it would be. I had already been informed my next destination was my home town, but it was a place I feared the most and didn't want that or anything else to spoil my hopes of happiness. I remembered nothing but the cruelty and abuse I once suffered there and the hungry cries from my younger siblings as they haunted me from time to time. The memory of the pains that gripped my stomach plagued my mind with the sexual abuse I often endured. I could scarcely forget the terrifying shadows that had once lurked around our dark and dismal rooms that now beckoned creatures of the night to taunt my mind with fear and sorrow. But because of this I was strong. I was no longer that pitiful child without hope. That part of my life had passed and young Molly had survived. It was her will that dwelt within my soul giving me strength to face the demons that had become a part of my life.

With the passing of years, I looked forward to my new start and wanted to make a go of it at Southgate House. I had thought many times about my home town but the very fear of it clouded the many memories I once had. I could remember so little of my early days or friends that no longer seemed part of my past, yet somehow the memory of Foxen Dam remained fixed within my thoughts just like a dream of yesterday, those beautiful sun kissed woods with the bluebell miles filled my heart with all the good things I had left behind, seemingly offering me a gift of hope for the future.

My first day back in Eckington was terrifying. I had the strangest feeling that my body had returned but my mind remained absent. It was the only defence I had when observing a situation I was unsure of, when the fear stored inside my heart caused my hands to tremble and filled my whole body with panic I switched off completely. Every sight and sound urged a nervous ripple throughout my soul, I knew right away that I wasn't ready for it but it was too late. I had now come face to face with my past and wondered if I could ever let anyone know that in my heart I was still crying, not for Marie but for little Molly who still remained soaked in guilt, searching for a way out.

It seemed I had now gone full circle. Once rejected by my own family I struggled with life hoping it would be kind to me but, nothing ever changed. The years I'd been away proved as difficult as the years I'd spent at home and now I was back to face the town that bore the knowledge of my abusive childhood, I now understood what it was like to feel doomed. With so many questions and answers to be given I faced a life of torment, and although I was certain of my childhood innocence it almost seemed that the town folk judged me guilty of my own fate. But, before I blamed myself for my family's destiny I thought long and hard of the desperation I'd once felt as a young and lonely child, knowing that while I had placed no importance in myself, I had cared for my siblings who, without me may not have made it. So my conscience was clear.

I believe it was fate for me to return to Eckington. Doing so gave me a realistic view of the town and its people and I was pleased I no longer felt a part of it. I thanked God I was merely passing through.

My memories of Southgate Children's Home are bitter ones, caused by the cruelty of Doreen and Dennis Wingfield, who found extreme pleasure in punishing me for being my Mother's daughter. They were principal staff of the home and made my life difficult thus giving me even more reason to lose faith in the human race. Their inability to accept me became obvious when they gave out detailed accounts of my family's background during moments of anger, making it known to others that my family name should be frowned upon and held against me. They gave me every reason to believe I shouldn't be accepted amongst the local community and plagued me with cruel thoughts and comments. I was constantly judged for the person I could have been as opposed to the person I was and each child that lived there allowed Doreen's personal thoughts to interfere with their opinion of me so making it difficult for them to befriend me. I was lonely and withdrawn and barely speaking to anyone, I lost all interest in myself and in my surroundings and cared nothing for anyone or anything. But it seemed fate always found a way! Having lost most of my inner strength it was fortunate my mother became aware of the Wingfields' biased opinions and somehow she managed to protect me.

Following a long and intrusive meeting, I was removed in the presence of a police officer. My social worker arranged a short stay at my sister's where I was asked if I would like to return to my mother's but by the time I'd been removed from Southgate House, my spirit had already been broken. I was cautious of everyone and didn't care where I was going, or what was happening to me. I had accepted that I was a far lesser person than anyone else, so it was no surprise to me that they were having difficulty in finding me a new home.

Mother lived alone, she had left Eckington after she had abandoned us, since then it became apparent she had lived a very lonely life. Yet she had found employment and managed to buy a small house to gain some stability for herself, but her life consisted of only two people, herself and her friend Joe, who had also moved away from Eckington to be near her.

When she was approached by my social worker, she instantly agreed to let me live with her but I was sure she only agreed because I was mature for my age and didn't need caring for. After all, I was well over the age of fourteen with an overall appearance of a mature woman, which I think gave Mother a false impression of my capabilities. I declared a preference to live with her rather than live at the girls' home for unruly children that I was threatened with. This was the day that The Derbyshire County Council failed me. I had experienced many difficulties in care. My inability to communicate was only one of them, I lacked so much confidence I couldn't think for myself and by the time I had figured out what they wanted from me, I was being humiliated and punished for being out of control. During the six years I had spent within the children's care system, I managed to relate to very few people and even when I did my response was so slow I was frowned upon.

—m—

CHAPTER 18

Returned to Mother

It was December 1972 and I was feeling rather excited about going to live with Mother. It was winter and the ground was thick with snow and just for that reason alone I was feeling on top of the world, it was just weeks away from Christmas and the buzz of the festive season spread happiness over people's faces.

I was so sure Mother would be as excited as I was but when the day came, I approached her house and I could see there were no flags flying to welcome me home. When my social worker's car pulled up outside 21 Empire Street, Mansfield, I climbed out hoping to see some kind of sign that would make me feel wanted but my disappointment had only just began.

I was standing at the side of the car waiting for my luggage to be piled into my arms when I realised the greeting I had expected wasn't what I had received, there were no happy faces, good will or Christmas cheer and the absence of my mother said it all. I had made my way back to her but, I was no longer sure it was what I really wanted. I couldn't understand why I felt a sense of rejection before I had seen her as I had been waiting for this day for so long, yet something told me it wasn't quite right.

I knocked hard on the bright yellow door and waited patiently for her to answer but after the third time of knocking I realised she wasn't at home. I looked up at the house as a sudden feeling of disappointment ran through the whole of my body, causing me to step back from the door. Taking a good hard look I admit the whole appearance gave me the creeps, it was definitely an older house, badly in need of repair and decoration, and even at my age I could see there was a lot of work to be done and couldn't understand why she had purchased such a rundown place. I gazed around at the neighbouring homes noticing that most of them where in peak condition, with freshly painted window frames and matching lace curtains in every window. It made me feel ashamed that Mother's had only a small piece of dingy grey netting stretched right across the bay window, making the appearance of the house look far worse than it really was. As my excitement drained away, I lowered myself down onto the wall that divided her house from the neighbours and let out a long extended sigh. My social worker stood close to me remaining very positive, she assured me things would get better, I wasn't so sure.

Mother eventually arrived on a motor scooter that she had specifically bought for travelling to and from work. She quickly apologised for being late then, disappeared down a long passage way that ran the length of the house, and within minutes she reappeared at the front door and holding it wide open she asked us inside.

My mood changed instantly from the disappointed little girl to the impressionable teenager I was. But when I entered the house I realised it was a step down from what I had been used to, it was the most dismal looking place I had ever seen. The rooms were almost empty with very little furniture and it was so dark I could barely see where I was going. I sensed a feeling of pride within my mother as she showed me around but I pitied her for the standard of life she had. Although she was more than satisfied with having her independence, I couldn't help feeling sorry for her. I suppose I complimented her in a way when I told her the house was pleasant. What I really thought lay in the pit of my stomach, churning over the memories of a similar place where we once lived with Father and nine of my siblings. Even after all those years it seemed she hadn't changed. Her standard of life remained much the same and I knew she wouldn't change. She had a strange way of turning a house into a cold unwelcoming shell; which made me feel I didn't belong.

I remembered that even as a small child our house was never a place I felt I belonged in, no matter what she did it always felt cold and empty, even the heat from the large open fires couldn't thaw the atmosphere she created. Until that day, I had forgotten the emptiness I felt when I was around her. Her dark and dismal rooms suppressed me with fear and I felt no different to how I felt back then.

Whilst I had no escape from a family that persecuted me, I felt my life was entering a period of solitude. Already I could feel the loneliness creeping into my soul as I searched aimlessly inside myself for some kind of hope for the future. I was kind, my heart was good and I would give my all just to please others but I asked myself were these the qualities I needed to survive amongst a family capable of squeezing every last drop of blood from my bones. I shuddered to think and trembled at the very thought of being one of them. In the forefront of my mind was a very faint memory of my sister Julie, her love and kindness was the only thing that seemed to separate good from evil. Although I remember each one of my siblings, I knew they created a devastating force that frightened me beyond belief. If not for her and my father, I could not have seen any good in my family at all. For a second, I panicked at the thought of my social worker leaving me behind but, as always, I remained strong. After all, I couldn't be seen to be weak particularly as I had a part to play. I was no longer a child society pitied, but was now recognised as a member of the Wass family. I knew I was never going to forget that.

It felt strange having to start all over again. I was approaching fifteen and only had a short time left at school yet there was so much I didn't know, and even everyday, simple things created problems for me and because Mother worked shifts, I had no one to teach me the things I needed to know. At times I felt just like a fish out of water. I relied on magazines and posters to show me how times had changed; everything I saw was different - buildings, clothes and even people had changed so much, I barely recognised it as the society I had been taken from.

Being alone, I spent most of my time cooking, cleaning and taking care of a house I found hard to call home. My days were long and lonely and stretched well into the night. Sleeping in an empty house terrified me, while Mother worked nights I trembled from head to foot as I chased dark shadows around the dismal rooms I had quickly come to hate. My fear of the dark seemed to make no sense as I loved the phenomenal night skies, they gave me such feelings of security and comfort, while a house without light represented everything that was hostile and gave me nothing but terrifying thoughts, thoughts that surfaced to the forefront of my mind.

My life had been tainted with a host of peculiarities and now it was left to me to try and turn a whole lifetime of mistakes into something good. The only chance I really had was to change who I was and so I began a whole new adventure.

My first thoughts were to change my name. Marie had never been a name I liked. I much preferred the name I grew up with – Molly. Molly was a great name but I feared for her, I couldn't take back her name any more than I could accept what had happened to her. I knew it wouldn't be right to bring her back from the past, it had been so long and there was no way I wanted to recapture her memories of rape and abuse. Her personality had been so strong yet I couldn't allow her to live here and now. To do so would have caused her a great injustice.

I recalled the song my Father lulled me to sleep with when I was young. Associating my name with this memory I realised that Rosemarie had been the name I was christened with and yet my family had chosen to disregard it. I had wondered many times why in all those years, none of my siblings or my mother had ever referred to me as Rosemarie. I couldn't think why and I am sure now there was no particular reason. But if it hadn't have been for my father, I'm sure I wouldn't have ever known my full name. For me Rosemarie represented femininity, a name that should have made me feel young and beautiful but I knew I was none of those things. Having suffered a life like mine it seemed to contradict my whole identity. Even though my imperfections gave rise to inadequacy, I liked the name; although at times I thought it was far too beautiful for me. It made me want to be all the things that I wasn't. I wanted to feel different and have a new name; a new name for a new life. My brain forged full steam ahead as I tried to create a master plan to build a new appearance to go with my new name.

Growing my hair was the first step. I had never been to a hairdressing salon so it was shoulder length already and almost black in colour. I regularly washed and brushed it to encourage growth, just as I had been taught whilst in care but I knew very little about make-up. I had seen women in old magazines and noticed a huge calendar in Mother's bedroom advertising life insurance. The model on the front page was seductively dressed in a long black cloak that flowed in the wind as she seemingly glided along a cliff-top. Her hair was tightly held in an oversized hood that allowed me full view of her exquisite features that were totally mesmerising. Her face lightened the darkened room and her mystery enthralled me. Then one day, I saw myself in her and I knew immediately I had put a deserving face to Rosemarie. I studied her make-up which was utterly flawless and after weeks of practise, I perfected the look of the 'Scottish Widow'. From that moment on, my make-up was my life and not only did it protect the youth in me but, gave me the confidence to discourage friendliness, giving me added protection against confident males. I didn't set out to isolate myself but knowing how vulnerable I was, I had found a protection that worked. Having been robbed of my virginity before the age of six, I knew no one was there to protect me, so I relied on no one but myself.

As I spent much of my time on my own, time passed slowly at Mother's, I noticed her life had not changed.

She thought nothing of finishing work then stopping off at her friend Joe's for a fish and chip supper, often returning home well after midnight. By which time I was in bed crying tears of self-pity and regret. Communication between us was poor and I began to wonder why she had taken me back at all. She reserved one Sunday out of four as her personal laundry day that gave us the opportunity to talk, but after being there for a few months, I had nothing to talk about and I felt isolated.

I began to wonder what life outside was really like, imagining more to it than I had ever dared to dream of before. The large bay windows that looked out on to the street gave me a pleasant view of illuminated homes, each one looking more inviting than the next but my confidence had been shattered many years ago, leaving me with the daunting thoughts of terrifying possibilities and because everyone was a stranger I feared the worst. Although I thought very little about it at the time, my anxiety of leaving the house had already begun. I knew it wasn't normal to worry and perspire at the thought of leaving the house, no more than it was to hide behind closed curtains all day long but as I never saw anyone, who was to know?

When I was finally enrolled in school I began playing truant but on Mother's day off when I had to attend I wrote my own notes to cover my absences. I found school difficult, it was mixed and some of the boys were over confident with girls they found attractive. I was often disciplined for defending myself against their suggestive insults so I found it easier to remain at home.

I recall a particular Friday when I'd been to school and was on my way home, a boy from my class became quite physical. He underestimated me. He approached me from behind, wrapped his arms around my chest and took a firm hold of my breasts, sniggering with pride as he thoughtlessly rubbed them together. I instantly turned to face him, gave him a hard slap on the side of his face and knocked him clean off balance. I was angry but felt more ashamed. I hadn't yet got used to having breasts so large and I felt embarrassed when he brought them to everyone's attention. He hurled the most abusive language at me to cover his own embarrassment as I walked away, leaving half the school laughing at him. However, the following Monday I wasn't surprised to be called to the headmaster's office where, after hearing both sides of the story, he gave me 200 lines of *"I shall not take the law into my own hands"*, whilst my assailant received only 500 lines of *"I will treat young ladies with the greatest respect"*.

I felt penalised by his decision as I considered myself the innocent party and the one most injured. It seemed this school was radically different to those I had been used to, I had spent most of my school days in small rural schools and had been taught respect at the highest level – something the Ravensdale boys didn't seem to know much about.

It was hard to accept, but I soon realised I was living among people of a different class, but try as I might I couldn't understand boys of this calibre.

—w—

CHAPTER 19

The Ruin of My Hopes

My life went from bad to worse. Mother spent more time away from the house and me and I spent more time away from school. The house became more like a den than a home and I began to feel frightened of a situation I couldn't make any sense of or understand. My time was my own yet I had nothing to do with it and I began to feel sad and lonely. I couldn't stop myself from crying and after weeks of hating myself, I made an appointment at our local surgery to see a doctor but when I got there I had no idea what to say. I wanted to tell him about my sad and bitter life and how it made me feel, but I settled for a sore throat, collecting any medicines they prescribed for me from our local pharmacist. Visiting the surgery gave me a feeling of acceptance and self-worth. I had somewhere to go, a purpose and being around people in a safe environment made me feel alive. The more regularly I visited the more confident I became until eventually I found myself making appointments just so that I could get out of the house.

It was some time before Mother was aware of my visits to the surgery but after one of my final visits, she had an irregular visit from Doctor Rogue who spoke to her in the most familiar way. I was curious about his reason for calling so I paid particular attention to the way he spoke to her but it seemed nothing more than a friendly call so, I accepted it as such and left the room without giving it a second's thought. But as he was leaving, I couldn't help noticing he put a strange kind of emphasis on my name as he called out goodbye. I thought it was peculiar but even so I assumed I was being paranoid and just ignored it. I walked from the front room to see him out and said goodbye, knowing Mother expected that of me. But when he arrived again the following evening, I began to wonder if Mother was ill.

I quietly pottered around the house watching for any tell-tale signs of a hidden illness but I realised after a while it was just another friendly visit. Eventually I convinced myself that as Mother worked with the elderly, she knew him. They seemed to get on quite well and I thought at some stage maybe he was smitten by her. So I was shocked to find, while Mother was out of the room, he moved up close to me and held my hand. The words he spoke were well above my head so I just stood there and let things happen.

Somehow I sensed he was seduced by my outward appearance and at that moment I was confused, I wasn't sure if he was my doctor, my friend or something more than that. I didn't fear him so I wasn't frightened to be alone with him; all I knew was that he was being kind to me and I didn't want him to stop. His hands were softer than my own and the sincerity I felt within his touch said it all. He loved me and I felt that pass to me. How it had happened I don't know but I was sure I could love him too.

I had seen him so many times at the surgery yet never once did he treat me disrespectfully. He knew me as Rosemarie and treated me better than anyone I had ever known. Just for a minute I felt totally engulfed in so much kindness and my whole world tipped upside down. While Mother was out of the room I felt the tenderness of his arms envelop me as he placed a gentle kiss on the right side of my cheek before he released me.

From that day on, whenever I was in his presence he bestowed so many compliments upon me I began to brim with confidence and felt remarkably special when he was around. He visited me every evening, showing regular concern for my health and welfare and encouraged me to attend school. He showered me with gifts and sweet smelling flowers, although I had so little to give him, he brought sunshine into my life where I had none.

For months our relationship was the only consistent thing I had in my life. He opened up my world, allowing me to see everything that was beautiful, turning my dull and insignificant life into something remarkable; he allowed me to feel undamaged and complete. I remember thinking to myself, if there was a cure for neglect and abandonment then this was certainly it. Any problems, doubts or fears that I experienced he set to right, minimising every worry I carried upon my shoulders. I saw him as a gift, something special. I didn't know where he was going or where he had come from but what I did know was that, just for that moment, he was mine.

He was someone I wanted to hold on to with all my strength, I wanted to love and hold him yet all the time I was with him strength didn't seem to be part of my anatomy. Time seemed to pass so quickly, learning as much about love as I did about life, but I didn't realise how quickly it was all going to change.

Mother came and went, doing her own thing, leaving me to live my own life while she got on with hers and sometimes I didn't see her for days. When she came in I went out, leaving her alone in the house as she did me. Occasionally I saw my social worker who tried to keep track of my life and encouraged me to communicate with Mother but regarding Mother I was hurting, I knew she didn't love me but trying to accept this as fact hurt me more than anything. Telling her I still loved her was impossible as my fear of being hurt was far too great and all my efforts were spent on trying to protect myself.

Eventually my suppressed feelings led to aggressive outbursts, causing our relationship to suffer. Then she did something I least expected. It was the one thing she knew would ruin my life. Why she did it I don't know. I could only suppose she was guided by the Devil himself. When she offered John a home in the same household it really sickened me, she couldn't have forgotten he had raped me as a younger child, so I was devastated by her decision to take him in. I cried myself to sleep most nights worrying about it, wondering what she was trying to do to me. I couldn't tell the doctor, I was too ashamed. Over the years I had found it almost impossible to tell anyone and felt really hurt that out of all Mother's children, I was the one he singled out. I had always wondered why it had happened to me and sometimes blamed myself but then I remembered I was just "The Child". I wasn't to blame!

Although John was one of my siblings, I was terrified of him. He had disrespected me so much over the years that at times I felt like cutting my life short, but born one of the weakest of Mother's children, I feared death too. I had no escape from him, there was no one to help me and it was my own shame that made me a prisoner of circumstance. Although I knew having courage to tell someone would have given me the protection I needed, for some reason it proved to be the most difficult task of my life.

Since attending school regularly, I had made friends with Denise, a young girl of my own age. She was pretty like me but livelier. We often spent time away from school on community work to help the elderly. It was something we had chosen for our work experience, knowing we could spend half the day away from class without getting into trouble for playing truant. Helping people to do their shopping was far more exciting and gave us a lot more freedom, so we really enjoyed it; until the day I saw John. It was the first time I had seen him since he had been released from prison. Although I was quite sure he wouldn't recognise me, I trembled at the slightest thought that he might. I was so frightened of him I walked the streets for hours before going home that night. When I finally found the courage I returned home only to hear Mother laughing at his filthy jokes, just as she always had.

I felt humiliated and went straight upstairs so that I didn't have to see him but, when Mother called me down I knew it was to tell me he was here to stay. I wasn't sure what she expected from me, so I just made it clear that I wouldn't tolerate his presence and I wouldn't give up my room for him. I couldn't help making it obvious that I disagreed with her decision to take him in, especially as there were only two bedrooms in the house, but I could see my words made little difference to either of them.

For weeks I spent all my time dodging around the house trying to avoid him but he had a disgusting habit of masturbating openly outside my bedroom door, knowing sooner or later I had to leave my room. It had happened so many times when I was a small child I had learned to take it in my stride, pretending he wasn't there. Even though I feared him, I ignored what I could. Sometimes I managed to get away with just a glimpse of him exposing himself but at other times I bore the brunt of a vicious attack. I informed Mother several times of his actions but for reasons I couldn't understand she was reluctant to believe me and I felt that I couldn't pursue it.

It had once been something I had endured every single day of my life but I had no intention of putting up with it again. I knew I was alone on this as Mother had always believed John's word above anyone else's so I struggled to fix the broken lock on my bedroom door and spent all my time nursing my sorrow behind locked doors.

Even going outside created a problem for me as he instantly followed me, creating a cat and mouse situation that petrified me. I hadn't found the courage to tell the doctor about him as I had already been branded an "abused child" all my life so I didn't want him to be blinded by my label. I desperately needed the doctor to see me as an equal, something I had never experienced until the day I met him. I wanted him to look at me with respect, my past was behind me and I didn't want it to flaw my future.

I managed to keep seeing the doctor even though John tried to ward him off. Since Mother had made John the man of the house he seemed to think he owned me but he was wrong. I had grown since he had been away and I was a little stronger than he thought. The doctor meant everything to me so I wasn't about to give him up on John's say so! He was my older brother but I had no respect for him and I hated everything he did. Just looking at him repulsed me. I wondered how it was possible for two men to be so different.

When I wasn't at school and Mother was at work, I found myself cooped up inside my bedroom, listening to the clock ticking away the hours until 5.30pm came around when the doctor finished surgery and he was able to pick me up. I couldn't wait to get out of the house; it felt like a prison although my fear of leaving it created worries too. I knew I was safe with the doctor, his understanding of the human race seemed to calm me and I loved him for it. Every night I promised myself I would tell him about John but my fear of losing him was far too great. He was the one person in my life I could trust and yet I couldn't trust myself to tell him.

Things became so bad between John and I, on occasions I had to phone Mother at work. His sexual fantasies got out of control resulting in him attacking me, tearing at my clothes like a mad man, trying his damnedest to have sex with me. I fought so hard that I shook with fear, wondering how I was going to survive and I cried for hours afterwards. What he was doing wasn't normal and because I was older now, I realised that, but I wondered would I always have enough strength to fight him off? I recall Mother's neighbour, Alice, blankly looking at me as I ran onto the streets desperately searching for help but never once did she offer me shelter; even though she heard my screams. I figured she was as frightened as I was. Being a woman on her own I knew she was just as vulnerable. The doctor was my only hope and I knew that if I couldn't bring myself to tell him, the day would eventually come when I would lose my battle with John.

Friday was Mother's last night at work before her two rest days so I knew John would try a lot harder to violate me. He seemed desperate to satisfy his own gratification before the weekend. He had made arrangements to go out socialising, knowing that alcohol gave him the excuse he needed to account for his behaviour but I made it clear, I would be going out myself and staying at the doctor's where I'd be safe. I had never stayed all night before so, it should have been a special night for me, a night I could have looked back on with so much pleasure but even that he had to spoil.

That evening the doctor made every effort to make me feel like I was the only person alive. I had known him for several months yet our relationship had remained one of innocence, until I felt a deep emotion to commit myself to him; fulfilling my need to be part of him. My instincts told me it was right, but later I wished with all my heart I hadn't seen him that night.

I have never forgiven myself for what happened next. As I lay at peace in the doctor's arms, I was suddenly woken by the sound of a deep thumping echoing throughout the flat. With such a commotion outside the window, I feared for the doctor's life as he hurried downstairs to answer the door. Following closely behind him I used his small frame to protect myself from John, who stood there in all his rage, shouting his usual abusive insults, first at me then, at the doctor. I was ashamed but too frightened to move. There had never been a moment in my life where I felt more strongly about killing him but my thoughts of harming him were interrupted by his aggressive demands to take me home. I was 15 years old and sensible enough to know he was only there to abuse me, so I chose to remain at the doctor's side. I knew John's cravings had overpowered his reasoning, creating an overwhelming need to fulfil his obsessive perversions and it was plain for the doctor to see that he suffered a dangerous desire to abuse me and would risk anything to satisfy his need for self-gratification.

I was so frightened, I shook uncontrollably. As I stood at the top of the stairs, I prayed that the doctor would have the sense not to let me go. As he turned and his eyes met mine, I knew he was there for me. Even John's constant threats of calling the police and having me removed didn't deter him from the decision he had already made. Neither I nor the doctor realised how much that night was going to change our lives. I had lived such an abusive life, I was older than my years, but I didn't realise my age was going to have serious repercussions for the doctor. I hadn't thought about being under-age and I knew he hadn't either. I was only weeks away from being 16 and far more mature than children of my own age, but John had worked it all out and that night we played right into his hands.

It was ironic really – if I had stayed at home that evening the outcome would have been very much the same but the police would have had to protect me from John instead of having to protect me from the only person I really cared for and who cared for me.

Although I could understand why the police arrested the doctor that night, I told them he was the only good thing I had ever had in my life and a person I really cared for. I couldn't understand why they kept him, leaving me to face the world on my own again. That night he lost everything, including his rights to practice medicine under the National Health Service, being charged with unlawful sexual offences against a minor; it not only ruined his life but mine as well.

I was devastated when he was arrested and even more so when I was removed from his flat and physically examined by his senior partner, Dr. Mc Sweeney, who verified that I had, in fact had sexual intercourse that night. I had been through so much rape and sexual abuse before that night I found it hard to believe that anyone could accept the damage I had suffered had been caused by him and him alone. I have never been able to understand what possessed John to do what he did that night. He was my brother but I suppose he hated me just as much as I hated him.

Eventually I was removed from Mansfield and taken back to Killamarsh to live with my sister Anne and her family where I spent most of my time trying to understand the logic of the law. I wasn't sure what hurt the most – having a loving relationship ruined by John or the mental torture of knowing that the only person that ever loved me was destroyed by who and what should have protected me.

—m—

CHAPTER 20

Shirley

It was a whole year before I saw Mother again, by which time I had left school and had found myself employment working as a shelf-filler in a supermarket at Eckington; the closest town to Killamarsh. At first I found it uncomfortable being back in my hometown again, but I had changed my appearance and had learned to behave differently, so found I was accepted with the greatest respect. I made every effort to keep my family's identity secret, knowing if I was ever recognised as a member of the Wass family I would be persecuted for it. I can't say I enjoyed my work but I lived day to day as if I was on cloud nine and thought about no one else but the doctor.

Living at Killamarsh I met my friend Shirley again, who I hadn't seen since she left Springhill that night. I was happy to see her as I had missed her so much. She was my best friend and had taken time to teach me lots of things whilst we were at The Outrake where we had lived side by side for several years. It seemed fate had separated us and brought us back together and we seemed to pick up where we left off. She didn't realise how much seeing her again actually meant to me but she was like a huge ray of sunshine, having a friend like her made my life a whole lot happier. I didn't speak to her about the doctor but something told me she already knew of him. Having had a traumatic childhood herself, she knew how important it was to be able to trust and so maintained discretion.

I was surprised to find she lived only a few miles away, close enough for me to visit. Although my sister Anne didn't allow me to socialise, I found she didn't mind me visiting Shirley occasionally, so long as I took one of her children with me. It was only half an hour's bus ride away from Killamarsh, so I saw her as often as I was allowed and as regularly as my money would stretch to the fare. I must admit I enjoyed the freedom of being away from Anne and all the housework and I got to be myself for a while.

Shirley's family knew me better than my own, having been brought up with them I didn't need to pretend I was somebody I wasn't and they didn't expect too much from me. My own family had a reputation and felt they had to live up to their name; they were tough, selfish and most of all, inconsiderate and I didn't like that.

Mr Bradbury, Shirley's father, was lovely; he seemed to be the perfect father. Having seen him most weekends at The Outrake, it almost felt like I was part of his family. I never knew why Shirley and her siblings were in care but when she finally told me that her mother had died, I was devastated. I couldn't understand why life had been so unfair, dealing the cruellest blows to the most innocent people. That night I cried for Shirley and her family and felt ashamed when I realised I had lived at her side for all those years yet knew so little about her. I suppose it was that that made me appreciate my own mother a little. As time went by, memories of the doctor slipped further away into the back of my mind but I still couldn't forget him. When I was alone I cried so much thinking about him,

I didn't think I would ever recover, remembering what he said to me when I last saw him plagued my mind so I knew I'd never forget him; being the kind of person he was made it difficult to forget him. He only ever thought of me, even at his most devastating time. He told me not to worry and stay strong but I couldn't, not without him. Even living miles apart didn't stop me from thinking about him and I knew unless I was able to forget him and move on, I would always be thinking about him.

Shirley and I remained close, going out together, trying to reshape our lives after a difficult time in care. We were almost sixteen yet had done so little since our release from the children's homes. We had made a couple of friends and remained very reserved, occasionally we ran into girls we knew from school but I noticed they seldom recognised me and only associated their past with Shirley. I felt quite pleased with that as I hated some of the memories I had of myself in school; I made the terrible mistake of becoming "the bully" instead of "the bullied" as I once was and because of that I felt ashamed.

In time Shirley met with a bus driver called John. Although she had had some innocent relationships with boys, I could tell this one was different. She spent most of her time with him, leaving me pretty much on my own, and although she tried to remain a faithful friend it seemed the progression of her own life interfered with the time she had for me and we began to drift apart. Seeing her only once in a while made me think more about the doctor and influenced my decision to return to Mansfield.

It had been 18 months since I had left Mother's and in that time my brother John had been sent back to prison for the usual sexual offences he committed on young women. I had heard a conversation between Anne and

Mother and discovered he had been given another four-year sentence for raping other girls soon after I left. I considered myself lucky at that point as I realised I had been kept safe for a few more years.

I was determined to leave my sister's house as I felt she abused my situation by insisting I help keep house for her and take care of her children while she went out socialising. She hadn't changed much over the years, she still found it difficult to put anyone before herself and because of the deceitful things she did and said I found I couldn't trust her. She was callous and cold and gave so little thought to my state of mind. She thought nothing of taking my wages each week, leaving me with only enough money to pay for my bus fares. I had very few clothes and just a single pair of shoes, all of which had come from the children's homes years previously. Any clothing the doctor had bought me was seized by the police and used against him as evidence. So when winter came and I was in need of a coat the social services arranged for me to go to the WRVS in Chesterfield, an organisation that clothed needy children like me. I was excited when I received the letter authorising me to collect a coat for myself from their stores, although it was old - fashioned and a little grubby it kept me warm and I was grateful.

Anne didn't want me to leave their house and I could see why, but I needed a more independent life. She had restricted my movements for so long I was beginning to hate her for it. Since I had found work I felt I was in a much better position to maintain myself, So I left with every intention of not going back.

—∿—

CHAPTER 21

Brian, My Mountain

Travelling to and from my job took hours so, I rarely saw Mother. After giving me a key to her house, she left me to my own devices and, as always, my life was my own. After settling in I began to change the house around, cleaning any mess left by John and tidying up after Mother. I opened up the curtains she insisted on keeping closed and redecorated some of the rooms to my own taste. Although she fought against every decision I made, eventually I managed to turn the house into something more homely.

Apart from a few pounds, all my wages were spent on items for the house, keeping it clean and maintaining its décor. But I couldn't impress Mother, our home wasn't important to her, whereas I wanted my home to be my castle.

Having very little time to myself, I found the memory of the doctor began to fade and I managed to get my life back together. I was only half way through my 16th year but I felt that I had lived many more years than that. I had already developed a grey streak in my hair so was obviously showing signs of decline but I felt privileged to have been born with such nice features which I believe

I made the most of. Although my clothes were important to me, I found I had so few in comparison to Mother yet I cared for mine to the highest standard, ensuring I was always clean and smart.

After developing a routine, I began to go out with my friend Brian, he was much older than me but he took care of things. With him, I felt I had no need to be sensible or mature, he knew I was a teenager and could be impetuous at times but he accepted that, I was young and wanted to have fun and there was no better person than Brian to ensure I did that. I saw him most nights after work and at weekends so most of my spare time was spent with him. He liked me so much, even my fear of crowded places didn't alter the way he thought about me. The time we spent together was always good, although much of it was spent inside his car, outside Mother's. Occasionally he took me to a country park and on Saturday nights he treated me to a meal. He was so considerate he searched the whole of Nottinghamshire for the most appropriate restaurant, knowing if it wasn't the right place I couldn't go in.

My life was different from previous years, I was almost carefree, I had stopped thinking about the past and cared nothing about the future, not realising the life I was choosing would have such bearing on my life in the future. I'd heard so many people say *"Life is what you make it"*, but I didn't believe a word of it. I had strong views on quotations like that and firmly believed that our families played a huge part in our destinies, even before we are born.

I felt my own life had been sacrificed from a very early age, giving others a chance to move forward and that my parents took little care of my early years, therefore providing me with insufficient knowledge to create a decent future, not only for myself but for any unborn children that I might have. But I remained hopeful. Brian taught me a lot of things and helped me to understand more about people, and although I knew I would never be anything special, I realised I was capable of doing better for myself than I had come to believe.

My relationship with Brian was nothing like the relationship I had with the doctor. Although we had something special I knew nothing would ever come of it. He was a good friend and occasionally a lover, but we both knew our lives would separate at some point. He spent a lot of time taking care of me and when my life went in a different direction to his, he was always waiting for me when I returned. He was a mountain to lean against and a shoulder to cry on, without him I would never have survived my teenage years.

—m—

~ CHAPTER 22 ~

Troubled Emotions

Life at Mother's was difficult. I found every single day a challenge, living in Mansfield and working in Eckington really had its downside.I remember freezing my hind off as I stood waiting for the number three bus to Sheffield. My nose had been running and I had suffered with a terrible cold but needless to say I still braved the bitter cold weather, I had to go to work. I had walked along Newgate Lane, over the iron bridge and followed the road round to the bus depot, trying all the time to avoid any other early risers who were also making their way to work. That way I didn't become subdued by fear.

When I left 'The Outrake' to move to Mansfield I had hoped I would like it there but I found the place daunting. It seemed so overcrowded to me and I often wished my social worker hadn't taken me to live there. When I first arrived I tried to look at things positively as she had advised me to but I felt so lonely and was sure that Mansfield wasn't the right place for me.

When I was small I had many dreams about the kind of person I wanted to become. I looked forward to having someone to confide in and something to believe in, although I understood very little of the kind of life

I yearned for. I could not free myself of the passion I had for the convents, from as far back as I could remember I had desperate hopes of entering a religious order as a novice and eventually living my whole life as a nun. For reasons I don't understand, I was enthralled by the mystery which surrounded the nun yet apart from their occasional presence on the streets, I knew very little about them.

I understood they had strict rules to abide by but I'd been so used to that, I knew I could have lived by them and the thought of giving up my family was a pleasurable one. Nothing I was told deterred me from wanting to become a nun. I didn't feel I belonged to the outside world, I felt different to everyone else so I looked for protection in something I thought I believed in.

In all the years I had been away from home no one had ever asked me about my thoughts on religion or what it was that I believed in and living at The Outrake for so long, I couldn't bring myself to speak openly about it or even confide in anyone. Once I had reached my teenage years I was so confused about life in general I kept all my opinions to myself and suffered the consequences, but eventually when I moved back home I confided in Mother. I found it difficult to approach her at first and felt uncomfortable discussing religion with her but then she surprised me by understanding my need to know more and openly informed me that my Grandmother had been Catholic and showed me her Rosary. It was kept in a brown triangular leather case and was in pristine condition. As she gently pulled it from its casing I remember thinking how beautiful it was, asking her what they were used for she said, "A Rosary is a series of prayers and the beads are for counting those prayers."

Her knowledge of the catholic church surprised me but then she went on to explain that it was only when she married Father, they chose to have us christened Church of England; that was my father's faith.

It seemed that from a relatively early age, all of us had had a mixture of religious cultures hurled at us, so by the time we had reached our teenage years we were as confused as one another but for reasons I couldn't explain, I had always felt Catholic. Maybe it was that, which set me apart from the others, knowing I was Catholic without having it thrust upon me. I believed in 'The Virgin Mary' and the 'Annunciation,' that's all I knew and all I felt I had to know.

I barely knew the history of my family or our ancestors so I wasn't sure whereabouts I'd come from or what religion I was supposed to be but something inside of me, told me I belonged to 'The Catholic Church'. I believed only in what felt right within my heart, and I felt Catholic. That explained why, from as far back as I could remember, I was drawn to the statue of 'Our Lady'. Then when I first moved to Mansfield she caught my attention again and I felt hypnotized by her. Although the outline of the Catholic Church was sometimes all I could see in the dark, I felt her presence within my heart and felt an overwhelming sadness when I had to leave her.

When the skies were clear, I often wept at the sight of her adorning the beautiful Church that I desperately wanted to see inside of, yet the strange thing was, I couldn't understand why. Being a child in care I couldn't even begin to understand my emotions but one thing I was certain of, if I was meant to believe in anything at all, it was her; I worshipped everything she stood for. I felt an overwhelming sense of innocence and purity when I was with her, she transformed all the hate I had built up inside me and helped me to feel hopeful again. When I was with her, I felt cleansed, different to how I felt when I was around Mother. Mother made me feel worthless and unclean. She made me feel more like her charwoman than her daughter. She had no qualms about coming home late at night, leaving her dirty clothes scattered around the house and dishes piled on top of the sink ready for me to wash. I tried to understand what I had done to deserve a life like that, but for all my soul searching I couldn't think of a reason.

Mother was a strange woman who thought everyone in the world was against her, insisting that nothing of hers was safe which resulted in every drawer, cupboard and door being locked with so many bolts and chains it would have taken a master locksmith to prise them open. I watched her closely as she crept around the house, hiding the food and clothes she thought might not be safe to leave out in the open. I often wondered if her life had been so bad that her mind wasn't what it should have been and sometimes I felt sorry for her. But then there were times when she had treated me with such disregard that I hated her. I treated this period of my life like a halfway point, knowing that eventually I would leave her.

Because I didn't really know what was expected of me, I felt like I was trapped. Since the day I had left the care homes I had listened to my social workers repeating themselves on how I should behave for Mother, but they showed no concern about the way she treated me. I never felt I could confide in them and found their interest in me had declined since I had returned home, so I found their visits somewhat wasted and wondered why they took the time to visit. It was only when I met

Mr Beresford, a new social worker that, I realised I had been rather neglected.

Mr Beresford was *"the perfect social worker"*. He first met me at Mother's when I was old enough to be smitten by his charm, he liked me and wasn't too shy to say so, which surprised me a little. I had accepted I wasn't always well liked and I could pretend it didn't bother me but his directness split my shell wide open and within a few weeks I found that despite his role in my life, I really liked him.

He was honest and supportive and I could talk to him like no other. He was the first social worker I felt I could trust and being a male, at first I was restricted in what I could say to him but soon found his unconditional ways relaxing and eventually looked forward to seeing him. He had the whole backlog of our family history and spoke quite openly about them but he didn't know as much as I did, although I was a little wary of telling him so. I knew that nothing I said was confidential so I kept my own counsel regarding a lot of things; remembering 'least said soonest mended'. In that way I knew Mother would never find anything out and I wouldn't be cross examined.

I had hoped maintaining a good relationship with Mr Beresford would in time guide me to something better but it was the same old devil that got in the way of my progress. I just couldn't get myself out into that big wide world without sensing fear and panic and couldn't find a way to discuss it with him. I looked so mature, I felt rather silly telling him I was frightened to go out on my own.

Mother had told him lots of things, including the fact that I had a boyfriend so he teased me regularly about it, hoping he could relax me enough to tell him more. But I was slightly more aware than he realised and wouldn't tell him any more than he already knew. To me his joking around just seemed a game, but to him it was a very important part of his work.

When I finally reached the age of seventeen, I realised my life wasn't going anywhere, I was miserable and felt such a failure. I had no qualifications and couldn't get another job, I was shy, lacked confidence and was ridiculously nervous and it seemed without a shining white knight in my life I was stuck indoors going nowhere. But what really hurt was that no one knew how desperate I was to move on. I had never been able to confide in anyone and apart from Brian I still couldn't trust anyone.

I was beginning to realise living with Mother was more difficult than I ever had remembered. None of my family had any respect for her and showed even less for me. Their visits to her house lasted only for a short while, just long enough for them to have a drink and a bite to eat and then they'd leave without a word of concern for me or Mother. They treated me like part of the furniture and Mother like a banker, never forgetting to press her for money before they left.

Mr Beresford was the only person I ever saw who took time to try and determine my physical and mental qualities, he showed me a lot of respect and in return I tried to give him the same. Sometimes I think he wondered what it was that made me tick, as I was the kind of person who remained reserved and kept myself cocooned inside a protective wall, where everyone around me was kept at bay. I remember him asking me lots of questions, some I even found quite personal and I was unable to answer those. I was so shy, I found it really awkward to hold a reasonable conversation and most of the time I spoke using only one word answers and reserved the right to remain silent when I didn't understand where he was coming from, but he was a patient man and very kind too.

I felt he understood me, and although I couldn't open up to him easily, he had a way of reading expressions that answered many of his questions without me uttering a word. I was grateful for that and offered him a smile when he got it right.

I hated it when people tried to force me to speak as it only served to block more of my thoughts making it even more difficult for me to hold a conversation. Being pressurised caused my mind to flick through memories of the past – it had been the same when I was a small child, cruelty, rape and abuse flashed through my mind creating fear and panic; the strongest emotions I had ever felt. I was seventeen but hadn't lived a single day without remembering the abuse and wasn't sure that I would ever get over it, but in all the years that had passed I couldn't understand why no one had ever asked me to talk about it. It seemed so long since it had happened yet, my memories of those terrifying days were still clear. I feared my past, so tried hard to forget it, hoping it would become easier to connect with the future, but the older I became the less I understood of the flashing images that constantly played havoc with my mind, like a video player stuck on repeat. The same evil scenes in the exact sequence they had happened taunted my brain bringing all the terrible memories forward from my past into the present. Sitting alone in my bedroom, I clearly remembered everything that had crippled my future:

Colour of paint, laugh or a giggle,
Spoken word, person's wiggle,
Fear of light, a sudden sound,
Little girl crying,
Tumbling to the ground,
Half bitten nails, porridge in a pan,
Broadened hands of a family man
Flower, clove, sweet smelling scent
Shrill of a bird, six coins being spent
Sound of voice, hammering on wood
Violet, Rose, a cow chewing cud
Dogs roaming free, wet patches of mud
Wiggly worms, christmas pud.
Sister, brother, friend or another
The smell of old clothes, someone's mother.
Car, sheep, a wellington boot
Single twist! of a liquorice root.

Strange as it seemed, it was those words that helped me to see that my troubled mind was that of an "abused child". I then understood that each one of those horrific scenes was a flicker of a second out of many hours of the pain and suffering I had had to put up with.

Still suffering the effects of abuse, I spent hours in isolation, troubled and lonely, my mind constantly flicking over previous scenes of agonizing torment; as my memory never failed to remind me of the life I had already lived. It was the fear of reality that locked me in a world of my own and no matter how much I tried I just couldn't free myself from it.

I had wished so many times that I had met Mr Beresford earlier, for the short time I knew him he seemed to play such a significant role in my life. I sensed and understood he was trying to help me, but the expectations he had of me proved to be too overpowering and frightened me more than I could say. I felt too embarrassed to tell him about my fears and the way they made me feel, so he never really knew me. He was unaware that the real me was a very different person to the one I had portrayed, but I was confident enough to know that he wouldn't spend time digging the real me from underneath all that heartache and sorrow. I knew I wasn't worth that much, not to him, not to anyone.

In all the years I had been under the care of the social services, no one had ever spoken to me about my past. I was never encouraged to talk about my family, my abusers or the time I had spent alone, yet I was crying out to do just that. I had wished so many times that Mr Beresford had guided me just that little bit further as there had been moments when I was so close to opening up but then he gave up on me. I had reached a point where I was willing to trust him but found it difficult to volunteer everything I wanted to tell him. I knew I was difficult to talk to yet my heart was begging him to drag those troubled memories from my thoughts. I would have done anything to rid myself of those haunting memories but, I didn't know how to make it easier for him. Having been the only male social worker I had ever had, I didn't think it possible to even look him in the eye, let alone talk to him but, as he showed more empathy than any of my female social workers, I sensed he had that special ingredient to gain an abused child's trust. I felt relaxed in his presence and more than willing to try and talk to him but somehow other things seemed to take precedence.

After my seventeenth birthday I began to realise that having only basic knowledge of maths and English was spoiling my chances of getting work. Despite Mr Beresford's confidence in me I was unable to fulfil the requirements that employers expected so I began to feel really ashamed of myself. It was only then that I realised how much schooling I had missed and began to regret ever playing truant. Although I knew I had never had regular schooling, I realised that by not attending when I should have, I had made things worse for myself.

Mr Beresford told me everything would work out fine but I didn't share his enthusiasm. I knew more about myself than he did and apart from my overall appearance and exquisite manners, I hadn't a lot going for me. I knew I hadn't enough educational skills to make anything of myself and at that time I hadn't even got the confidence to pretend I had. I had a really tough time trying to convince him that I hadn't the ability to walk down the street and land myself a job like other teenagers could but he was so hard to convince, it just made me feel even more hopeless.

By the time I realised the rest of my life wasn't going anywhere, I learned that proving my worth to strangers was the hardest job of all. I knew I had to find work but until I could free myself of the fear I had of people, I was incapable of doing anything.

Mr Beresford continued to visit me about once a fortnight but began to doubt that I was making any attempt to find work. I hadn't made any progress in either field and was just floating at a loose end. Surprised at his mistrust in me I instantly produced a barrier to protect my feelings and although I remained polite and respectful to him during any following visits, from that day on, his mistrust had lost me.

My older brother Trevor moved into Mother's house and gave my life a boost. We got on well and shared a lot of the same interests but even so it seemed having spent time in care he had also developed phobias of going out alone. From the moment he moved in, we were like two peas in a pod and our lives seemed to swing for a while. But then along came reality and spoiled it all. We shared the chores while Mother was at work, but it never seemed enough for her. She expected a lot from a couple of teenagers who had been in care half their lives.

As the children she abandoned we had nothing to give, apart from time and labour that she drained from both of us. Even then it wasn't enough for her, arguments occurred regularly between all three of us, until eventually I decided it was time for me to leave.

I had no other place in the world to go but I was determined I wouldn't stay. I was convinced she hated me and no longer wanted me around, so I planned to leave that same evening. While I was reading the Evening Post, I came across a vacancy for a childminder printed in the Personal column, I was so angry I telephoned and arranged an interview before I had even thought about it. That same night I walked away from her house to fill a vacancy I so desperately needed.

—⁓—

CHAPTER 23

A Special Phase of My Life

I was finally out on my own, without a penny to my name, heading for the City of Nottingham. Luckily the money Trevor loaned me paid for my bus fare and before saying goodbye he made me a firm promise that he would never tell a soul where I had gone. I felt sad at leaving him, it reminded me of the night I left him behind when we were younger children yet I had never felt such relief as when the bus pulled away from the stop.

I was heading for the White Hart at Daybrook, which for me was an unknown destination so I was pleased when the driver agreed to put me off at the right stop. I couldn't believe I was on my way to meet someone I didn't know. The only thing I knew was the gentleman's name and the type of car he drove, but when I spoke to him over the phone he sounded genuine so, I went along with my instincts hoping my decision was the right one. He offered to meet me at the White Hart which saved me 30 minutes travelling time and a little of Trevor's money, which I considered helpful. Although I was worried about getting the job, my fear of going out and meeting people disappeared beneath the anger I felt for my mother. As I travelled down to Nottingham I realised for the first time in my life, I was now, really all alone.

I remember arriving in Nottingham at 8.30pm. It was dark and as I stepped from the bus, a blizzard of oversized snowflakes fell from the sky clouding my view of the White Hart Hotel. It was just as it sounded, white, but gloriously lit by coloured lights. As the snow settled on my long, dark hair I suddenly realised I was totally free. I stood at the bus stop brimming with excitement as I watched my warm breath hit the cool crisp air, turning it into a cloud of vapour before it disappeared. I felt a surge of excitement run through me as I gazed at all the snow that had settled on the ground. I was motionless, although I wanted to move, the overall sight of a beautiful winter's night overwhelmed me. I looked for the gentleman who had described himself as being of medium build and smartly dressed, but the neighbourhood was desolate. As I walked across the road my eyes searched the hotel's car park for a red estate car, hoping the puffs of vapour coming from a vehicle's exhaust, would be his. As I approached the car I realised the driver's window was open so headed towards it, hoping my intuition was right. When I got close I could see a gentleman sitting, snugly wrapped in a dark overcoat. He pushed open his door immediately and emerged from his seat repeating my name. I smiled to reassure him that I was the one he was waiting for. Quickly introducing himself, he shook my hand and gave me his full name. His demeanour was one of a gentleman, which instantly put me at ease.

Although we seemed to fit into each other's company quite easily, I wasn't sure at that point whether I was the kind of person he had expected. His priority at that moment in time was to get me out of the cold, once I was tucked into my seat he chatted openly as he drove carefully to a small country restaurant for an informal interview. My mind was so set on getting the job the fear I would normally experience was overpowered by the threat of failure. I was desperate to get away from Mother's and this was my only chance. I was dreading him seeing me in the light as I had already lied about my age and wouldn't have known what to say had he asked me again. I was sure I could pass for being older but I wasn't too keen on lying to him. I had this strange notion that if he knew I was only seventeen he wouldn't consider me able to care for his daughter. I had almost denied myself the position before the interview had started and worried myself sick at the thought of not getting it.

It was about 20 minutes ride to the quaint restaurant he had chosen and as we arrived he asked if I thought it acceptable. I don't think I had ever seen such a beautiful place. It was situated way out in the country and I became quite excited as he drove the car into a space at the front of the foyer. He wasted no time emerging from the car, opened the door at my side and then stood back, allowing me to move forward and lead the way. I told him it was beautiful and more than ideal. He moved in the most dignified manner, never forgetting to consider me before himself. As we approached the building, we hurried indoors shaking off the cold, crisp snowflakes that covered our clothes. Forgetting myself, I gave out a playful giggle as he brushed away the snow that had settled on my hair but he smiled as he joined in my excitement. Somehow my childish ways broke the ice and the evening turned out to be one of the happiest of my life.

I experienced a lot of things for the first time that evening and enjoyed everything about it. The gin and tonic I drank no doubt had quite an effect on me, being a non-drinker, I was a little tipsy after the first. But I must admit I had never felt better. I'm not quite sure whether it was the effect of the drink but I found I could speak quite openly to Roy. He was 26 years my senior yet, I felt amazingly at ease with him. The evening ended back at Bestwood Park. He had a beautiful home, though it seemed rather large for just him and his daughter. He suggested showing me around while Cheryl was away and volunteered to drive me home afterwards. I knew no one was waiting up for me so I accepted his invitation and felt confident I was doing the right thing. I was so sure it was a sign I had earned the position of childminder, so I just relaxed and went with the flow.

I assumed he made coffee in an attempt to sober me up, which I drank while talking and listening to some background music. I had never heard of Barry White but strangely enough his music seemed appropriate.

I was eager to look around and gently prompted him, the house was of a much higher standard than I was used to yet, I didn't feel out of place. Once I had seen the front and back of the house, he led me to the bedrooms where we spent a considerable amount of time in the spare room, it was full of collectables and unusual objects of bygone days. The small, wooden gramophone took my sole attention as my father used to have one just like it. I asked him to play one of the old 78rpm discs from the neat pile at the side and without hesitation he obliged. The exquisite voice of the Italian baritone Mario Lanza singing 'Ave Maria' was the most beautiful part of the evening. Roy had brought to mind one of the very few happy memories of my childhood and as my mind swayed from the present to the past I visualised Mother and Father at their happiest and I cried.

Roy was a gentleman, he spoke very easily to me, was polite and eager to please so I suppose it was inevitable that we would get on. As we left the spare room, he casually asked if I would like to stay the night. Leading me into his daughter's room he suggested I could sleep in there. Finishing the tour we returned to the lounge where I made the decision to stay. I didn't really want to go home, so it didn't take me long to make up my mind. Cheryl's room was exceptionally feminine and looked so inviting. It had the beautiful aroma of Avon's peach blossom and it was obvious by the little bottles of children's perfumes, she was regularly adorned with such gifts. I was tired and didn't care for the 2 - hour journey it would have taken to get back to Mother's, so I prepared myself to stay.

I remember it being around 4.30am before we finally retired. I was used to late nights but, I think the gin had relaxed me so much all I wanted to do was sleep. I'm not quite sure what happened next but I remember allowing him to guide me up the stairs towards his bedroom. My heart beat rapidly as the thought of sleeping with him even excited me. I knew what was going to happen but I hadn't the will to stop it.

That night changed me completely. It was the beginning of a special phase of my life. Although I wasn't sure what the future had in store for me, I was more than willing to trade my past for the future. I made up my mind to tell Roy the truth about my age and decided the following morning was the right time to come clean. I explained very warily that I was seventeen not eighteen as I had said, certain I had spoiled everything, but he assured me it made no difference. I was confused at first but then he explained that although he hadn't planned on sleeping with me, it happened because we wanted it to. He said it meant a lot to him and although he had always been sceptical about love at first sight, he was certain he was in love with me. That night I became "The Childminder" and Roy's lover and in time I found he made me feel happier than I had ever felt before.

I found life with Roy and his daughter exciting but eventually the security of their family life stifled me. I knew he cared for me but I found it hard to believe he could love me and although I felt something for him, I couldn't understand what those feelings were. I don't really think I knew what love was, as the feelings I had experienced with the doctor were quite different to what I felt for Roy. I was confused and struggled to understand emotions and because of that, I failed drastically in relationships.

Although he asked me many times to marry him, my understanding of marriage was not at all clear so I couldn't see any point in it. My continuous refusals became harder for him to accept and our relationship began to suffer for it. I tried to make him understand that marriage meant nothing to me but he seemed to take my continual refusals as rejections. I didn't intend to hurt his feelings but it seemed no matter where I went or what I did, I was hurting someone.

Roy and I stayed together for over two years. But despite what we felt for each other, we both found comfort in someone else's arms. I'm not sure who wandered first; I always surmised I did, although I sometimes wondered if he was far better at being deceptive than I was. It was difficult to understand what kind of relationship we had, for although he said he loved me, he treated me no different to his daughter. He failed to understand what my needs were and that I needed more than that. As his lover I was given unlimited boundaries, where my role was made quite clear but once I left his bedroom I felt like a protégée, defenceless and weak. His daughter treated me like her playmate rather than a carer and that made me feel vulnerable, a feeling I hated. The circumstances reminded me of my early childhood where at one stage I was just a little girl and then overnight I was turned into a sex object. I needed to rid myself of the memories I had of my abusive childhood but with constant reminders of little Molly's suffering, I found it difficult to move on. I wanted to talk to Roy but I feared it was something he wouldn't want to hear so it made it even more difficult for me to confide in him. I needed to rid the ghosts that haunted me but without anyone to turn to and nowhere for them to go, they remained trapped within me.

I was desperate to turn my life around so I found myself a job in a factory, hoping the hard work would help me forget where I'd come from, but my inability to cope with extreme heat finally made me so ill I had no choice but to terminate my employment. I must admit I wasn't sorry to leave Steibles. The women who worked there were less than friendly and made my stay much more difficult than I had ever anticipated, despite being warned of their uncongenial ways before I got there. I left only six weeks after I'd first started with very little experience but, I still managed to come away with a good reference which enabled me to obtain work at Fred Hartley's in Sherwood. I was glad of the move, I didn't like factory work and thought my time there was wasted but when I started work at Fred Hartley's I was over the moon. The staff behaved differently and seemed a little more reserved so, it seemed I fitted right in. I hadn't been there long when I realised I was being pursued by a rather exuberant young man named Terry. He was a lot younger than Roy and worked for the Corporation bus company. He was the typical tall, handsome type who brimmed with confidence and although I found him very attractive, it had never occurred to me to deceive Roy.

Terry had a lot of good qualities and over a period of time I got to know him quite well. I was impressed that he volunteered most of his spare time to the fire brigade in Arnold so I couldn't help thinking he was a little bit special. I began to look forward to the lunchtime visits he made to the shop but I regularly refused his offer of lunch, before eventually accepting the lunch date that led to many more.

Considering the time Roy spent in other women's company, I believed having lunch with Terry was justified, although I hadn't anticipated having a relationship with him. I spent a lot of time reasoning with myself until I was finally convinced I was doing nothing wrong. I wasn't married to Roy, I was no longer in the care of Social Services and I didn't feel I had to make excuses for my behaviour, so I carried on seeing Terry not realising Roy's jealousy would spiral out of control when he found out I was being entertained by another man. It wasn't long before my final lunch date with Terry came to an abrupt end when Roy forced his way into the Sherwood Arms brandishing a large carving knife in an attempt to kill me. I was terrified, I couldn't believe from all the rage and hatred I saw in this man's face that it was the same man I lived with. Despite the fact that he loved me, he was still willing to kill me.

My fear of him immediately changed everything. I ran from the pub as fast as I could without looking back and cried, as the very thought of him hating me sank deeper and deeper into my mind. I left him that day, knowing it was the best for everyone. I made a quick phone call to my friend Brian and he bailed me out of a relationship I thought I was in for life. I was almost nineteen years old and although I realised going back to Mother's was probably the biggest mistake of my life, I had nowhere else to go. Leaving Roy meant I had to give up my job which left me without income. I was no longer under a care order so was unable seek help from Social Services so, I had no choice but to sign on unemployed and receive dole money that was barely enough to live on. Once I'd settled, I searched all Mansfield looking for a job but it seemed I was never to have much luck in that town.

Roy knew I'd have difficulty if ever I left him and told me so frequently. But I had been determined to prove him wrong.I was stubborn but very often found that my stubbornness got in the way, I was young and felt I had to prove my abilities whatever the consequences. I knew I would always be indebted to Roy, if only for rescuing me on that cold winter's night; I was seventeen years old, without a friend in the world. I'd experienced nothing but heartache and fear. I was facing a whole new way of life, I depended on him. He didn't only become my lover and my friend that night but my guardian as well. When he met me, he took on far more responsibility than he realised, and although I had a lot of affection to give, I leaned heavily on his shoulders. Being an "abused child", no relationship came without extended problems and every emotion I had was built on cruelty, neglect and abuse. Although I radiated warmth and affection, I allowed no one to pass through my protective barrier.

As usual, my friend Brian picked up the pieces and helped me through a terrible time, the one thing I had with him was reliability. I had known him for so long he had become my best friend. Although we occasionally did sleep together - it was more for comfort than for self gratification. I had strong feelings for him but again I couldn't identify them. I felt good when he was around and enjoyed occasional sex with him. But strangely enough, when it came to kissing and caressing, it was more personal than I wanted it to be. For me caressing reached the heart of my soul and was reserved for people I thought very, very special. I had always found that kissing released my truest inner feelings and within the power of a kiss, I had no call for words.

I still got on with Brian although, he regularly pointed out that I had changed. It had been two long years since we had seen each other so it was inevitable he would notice some changes. I had toughened up and Brian thought it strange that I was able to go out alone. I still had a problem with crowded places but I wasn't as nervous as I used to be, I still clung to him but didn't rely on him as much. I carried on seeing him as I always had and occasionally he stayed the night at Mother's, knowing I was lonely. I hated being in the house on my own, he knew that and was company for me and because I confided in him, I learned from him. He told me many times that life was short so I should live it to the full and never be frightened to speak out. He said I was capable of doing anything; I so desperately wanted to believe that.

I think he knew life would eventually take me away from him but because he loved me, he didn't hold that against me.

—⁓—

Afterword

When I first started writing this book my most conscious thought was to protect the reader from any unnecessary trauma. Then I realised that after all this time I was still trying to protect others from the shame and embarrassment I myself felt as a result of the gross invasion I encountered as a little girl, and that wasn't the purpose of writing it.

When I met my counsellor he encouraged me to write and at first I thought it was quite absurd. I could barely read and had lost all my concentration so the last thing I wanted to think about was my abusive childhood, but Clive had put so much effort into bringing me back from the anomalous world I had entered into; I felt I owed him something. Over a period of time I managed to write a jumbled - up mess and I thought it would take me years to sort it all out ; I was right. Three years down the line I'm still struggling to find the right words to describe how it felt to write my story and what I feel now that these chapters of my life have come to a closure.

It is difficult to recall what I was really like when I started writing, as I was so ill I barely knew my own name. I'd heard many mothers say they were suffering a breakdown when they were experiencing difficult times with their children or when there was never enough money to last the week, and like most people I put my own interpretation to that statement, but now I know that suffering a breakdown is far worse than anything I had ever imagined.

Writing Molly has been a great experience for me; although I shed many tears on this emotional journey I would like to think I broke even with the occasional smile.

Remembering my past has clarified lots of uncertainties that arose during my childhood and I can only thank Clive for helping me to unleash the most frightening experiences of all. I have now come to terms with who I am and have learned to like the person I have become. I see the world as a more profound place and accept others for who they really are. Unlike most, I have learned not to shy away from counselling but to treat it as an education. I had always wanted to tell my story but had never found anyone strong enough to motivate me. Then suddenly I came face to face with Clive Powell who became my mentor as well as my counsellor and with time I gained enough confidence to enable me to fulfil a dream.

I have only one regret in life ; that I did not seek help before. It never occurred to me before now just how many people were affected by my abusive childhood and although I'm not trying to avoid taking responsibility for my own actions, I do think that all the problems in people's lives that have been caused by my own difficulties could have been avoided had there been a chance for me to receive long term counselling when it was needed most. As far as I am aware there is still no specialised medical or supportive care available to assist in our rehabilitation, for example, long term counselling - psychiatric help for children who suffer child abuse. So above all else, I'm hoping Molly raises awareness for children who have been mentally, emotionally and physically affected by the trauma and total devastation that abuse has had on their lives.

—⁓—

Clive Powell

Counsellor and Mentor

I am very proud to be asked to write a few words for Rosemarie's book 'Molly'. 'Molly' grew from Rosemarie accepting a challenge to write a personal journal as part of a therapeutic journey.

Choosing to work through issues that have plagued your life, through traumatic memories and emotions is a difficult decision for anyone to make and the journey will present the individual with many challenges. Some of the challenges may push you to face up to yourself, may change your perception of your life and of those people involved in your world. Rosemarie accepted these challenges.   I feel privileged to have been a witness to Rosemarie's journey of discovery, a journey that at times resembled a roller coaster ride through many emotional ups and downs. The way in which Rosemarie committed herself to her writing and working on the issues in between sessions has contributed to the wonderful book 'Molly'.

I sincerely hope those of you who read 'Molly' will find something in Rosemarie's words and very personal story to encourage you to consider embarking on your own personal journey of discovery. Everyone has a story but Rosemarie has chosen to write her story down, will some of you who read Molly's story be able to draw inspiration from Molly and her personal struggle to begin your own journey ?

Congratulations Rosemarie, you are now a published author and I look forward to reading the next part of your story. Clive Powell.

www.ingramcontent.com/pod-product-compliance
Lightning Source LLC
Chambersburg PA
CBHW031946080426
42735CB00007B/284